1

The Complete Kinnie Wagner Story

Preface

Tales of the "Roaring Twenties" are usually thought of as taking place in Chicago or New York, but some of the most exciting events occurred far away from the big bursting cities.

Influenced, perhaps, by the violence of war only a few years previously, when life was held by a happenstance of fate, some young individuals took to guns and crime as a way of life, and survival.

From those years came bank robbers like Bonnie and Clyde, John Dillenger, the infamous Touhey Gang, Baby face Nelson, Pretty boy Floyd, Clarence Bunch and others.

But these lawbreakers were motivated only by the greed for money, riches gained by stealing or killing, and the high life such wealth could bring.

This book is about another kind of outlaw. It is about a man who, had circumstances been different, could have been known far and wide as an expert marksman and trick shot artist.

According to his own story, Kinnie Wagner's troubles began with an unjust sheriff and a set up shooting that was supposed to result in his death and silence his criticisms of the law official.

But Wagner was a better shot, and his opponent fell dead.

Enraged, the lawman charged the young circus performer with murder and planned his execution. But Wagner escaped, and fled toward his native South Western Virginia.

The angry sheriff issued a Thousand Dollar Dead or Alive poster and offer for "The Killer" and sent it all over the south.

Perhaps as a result, Kinnie Wagner was accosted by five armed law officers, who, witnesses said, came shooting at him from three directions. Wagner shot back, and a life of killing and prison and escapes began for the man who would be called the fastest gun in the South

During his half century newspaper career, Pete Dykes collected stories and yarns galore from individuals who claim to have been witnesses to events. Whether these stories are true or mere folk tales, they are interesting and very well may have happened.

To retell the stories in readable form, the author chose to write in the person of Pug Potter, a character created for this specific purpose.

The facts contained in this story are all accurate, as taken from newspaper accounts of the day and from a number of individuals who have recounted their memories over the years.

Originally written as a continuing series for the Daily News of Kingsport, "Pug Potter's Journal" ran for several years. This book is taken from that series, and presents a great nostalgic view of a time now long gone but not forgotten.

The Complete

Kinnie Wagner Story

From *Pug Potter's Journal*
By Pete Dykes

Published by
Pete Dykes
310 East Sullivan Street
Kingsport TN 37660 USA.
All Rights Reserved.
ISBN 978-0-6151-5243-1

Trouble and Kinnie Wagner

When Charlie Houser, the pressman at the local newspaper, told me he might need me to come by and help him haul a load of paper from the depot that day, I never suspected so much excitement would come to our little town.

The town is Kingsport, by the way, in East Tennessee just barely across the Virginia State Line. It was still a new town in that year of 1925, having been incorporated as a city only eight years earlier, in 1917.

A scant twenty years ago, there was little more here than hills and trees and a river running down the valley at the foot of a mountain. And a railroad. Don't forget the railroad, because that's what made the town in the first place.

When George L. Carter, the entrepreneur of the Blue Ridge Mountains at the turn of the century, decided to build what later became the Clinchfield Railroad, a track that he hoped would span all the way from the Atlantic Seacoast to Chicago (it never did make it that far, running from Spartanburg S.C. to Elkhorn City, Ky. at its completion) he got a group of rich New Yorker bankers to put up most of the cash for the project.

The bankers sent one of their number, J.C. Dennis, down to the East Tennessee hills to watch out for their interest, because they suspected that ol' George L. was smart, alright, but that he might be a bit tricky when it come to spending their money, and they wanted to make blamed sure it went the way they thought it ought, instead of otherwise, like they figured it might.

George L. had hired his banker in-law, J. Fred Johnson, who had just got kind of shifted out of a bank he had an interest in over in Johnson City, twenty odd miles to the south of what was to become our town...George L. hired Jay Fred and sent him over to look out for HIS interest. Jay Fred built a "commissary" or store, and then got in with Dennis, and next thing you know, he is working for the New York bankers, who set up an outfit called The Improvement Company to take care of the land they had acquired. Oh. I forgot to tell you about that.

Dennis stopped in at a train station and telegraph office to send a wire one day, about 1908, when the railroad had got part way over through Virginia. The place he stopped off at was just across the state line in Tennessee, and he liked the looks of the land.

"This would be a fine site for an industrial city" he said to himself. A few days later, he said the same thing to the other directors of the Blair Company, the banking group he worked for.

They agreed, after checking things out, so they sent land agents to East Tennessee and bought up all the land, then hired Jay Fred to resell it and make a city of it.

A well-known city planner, John Noland, was hired to design a city. He laid out a design for a broad street running from the Clinchfield Depot to a Church Circle, indicating that the whole town should be between God and the Clinchfield Railroad, which it was, for a long time.

My name is Pug Potter, and I make my living by hauling things for people in my truck or one of my two cars. Sometimes I do odd jobs, like hauling people around for Jay Fred or other folks, not so much as a taxi service, but more of a guided tour, because I know the whole area around town. By 1925, our little town was becoming a boom town, because Jay Fred had persuaded George Eastman, the New York camera and film tycoon, to buy what had been a wood alcohol plant built by the government, but never operated, during the big war a few years back, and it had become Tennessee Eastman, and was hiring a good many people from all over the area.

When word got out that Eastman had jobs for mountain folk, they came in droves to see if they could get one of them. Folks camped out in an old orchard near downtown, building shacks out of cardboard and tar paper until they could find a better dwelling, and the town really grew fast.

Jay Fred had persuaded a lot of businesses and stores and such to come to our town, too, on the strength of workers at Eastman having paychecks to spend, and that made more jobs, of course, because somebody had to work in the stores and such as well as at the plants.

On that April day, just past Easter, the sun was shining and it was warm and nice.

I got in my truck and drove over to Market Street, where the newspaper plant is located. I call it a plant, although it is just an old store building, with the pressroom on one side and the office on the other, but it serves, I reckon.

Charlie was standing in the doorway of the pressroom when I drove up.

"I've been looking for you," he called out. "You ready to go get that paper for me?"

"That's what I'm here for," I told him. "You want to go get it now?"

"Might as well," Charlie said.

He had one of them little square caps he folds up out of newspapers on his head to keep the ink out of his hair. He pulled it off and tossed it down on the seat of a straight-backed chair that was there near the door.

We got into my truck and drove down Market Street a few feet, then turned right on to Broad Street and traveled the long block down to Main Street, where the Clinchfield Depot stands.

The paper was in big flat cartons, and there were a half dozen of them. We loaded it on the truck and got ready to take it back, but Charlie suggested that we step over to Shaffers Restaurant, just across the street, and have a cup of coffee.

Well, that suited me fine, so that's what we done.

We left the truck parked at the depot and walked across to the restaurant, which is just a few doors down Broad Street. There's a drugstore on the corner of Main and Broad. Doc Tipton owns the building, and has his office upstairs. That makes it pretty much of a sure fire success for the druggist who runs it, because Doc writes out a lot of prescriptions for his patients, and the druggist down stairs is the only one who can read his writing.

Next door there is a fruit-stand-news-stand-beer-stand sort of place, called the Fruit and News, and then the restaurant is next.

We went inside and sat down in one of the high backed wooden booths.

After the waitress came over and brought our coffee ... they don't ask you what you want if you are a regular, they just go on and bring it ... we sat there and sipped and talked.

Charlie asked me about the airplane ride I had taken a few weeks back, when this barn-storming pilot landed his little Jenny down on Sullivan Street flats near Reedy Creek, and I told him as best I could. I had been so excited and so danged frightened at the time, I couldn't remember much except how people looked kind of like ants way down below.

That all happened on account of I helped the pilot fix his plane, which was kind of broke down when he landed it, and he wanted to reward me for my efforts. That kind of reward might be alright for

11

some folks, but next time I think I'll settle for a warm smile and a word of thanks, and not get so sick to my stomach.

"I'm going to get me an airplane one of these days," Charlie said.

"You mean you want to fly?" I asked him.

"Why not?" he grinned. "If these other fellers can do it, I don't see why I can't."

He did, too, a few years later. Charlie was a kind of adventurous sort of fellow. He had motorcycles and boats and that plane and all kinds of things in the fullness of time.

He said he had been talking to a local boy, Rogan Showalter, who was learning to fly an airplane, and that Rogan said there wasn't much more to it than driving a car. Rogan had made friends with a stunt flyer who once landed over on Long Island, next to our town, and his new friend was teaching him to fly. If he gets to where he can fly one of the things, Rogan will be famous all over again, I guess. He got famous once, when the big war started, by being the first man in Sullivan County to volunteer for the army. Got his picture in the newspaper and everything. The Bristol paper, too, the one most people read.

There is a newspaper in Kingsport, but it don't amount to much. Tom Pratt and Howard Long keep trying to get it going, but it never seems to amount to much. They bought it a few years ago from that fellow Kincaid who started it, back in 1917, and he had it going pretty good as a weekly, so Howard and Tom figured they'd make a daily newspaper out of it and get rich, but nobody else around here seems to have had the same idea. They print it about every day, if they've got enough paper and ink, but it don't usually have much in it, and not many people buy it.

Charlie is the pressman. He had bought a big press when he got out of the army at the end of the war, and got into the printing business, turning out circulars and such, then when Pratt and Long bought out Kincaid, the old press he had broke down and they couldn't get it fixed, so they had to get Charlie to print their paper, and they finally just bought his press and made him their pressman to keep doing it.

"Say, Pug," Charlie asked me, "have you heard anything about that reward the folks down in Mississippi are offering for that Wagner boy?"

That was the second time in two days somebody had asked me about Wagner, and it kind of got my interest roused.

"No," I told him, "I haven't heard nothing about it. What kind of a reward?"

Charlie leaned back in the booth and lit his pipe, which took a minute or more. He puffed smoke at me for two or three times until he got it going just right, then he shook out the match and dropped it into a glass ash tray that was on the table of the booth.

"We got a letter from the Sheriff down in Greeneville, Mississippi," he said. "They are offering a thousand dollars for the capture of Kinnie Wagner dead or alive. They say he killed a deputy sheriff down there last Christmas."

"A thousand dollars? That's a lot of money!" I exclaimed. "For that kind of cash, I might capture him myself if I happened to see him!"

"They say he is a crack shot," Charlie went on. "And can shoot a pistol with either hand. Since he is wanted for killing a man already, he might be kind of hard to handle."

"Oh, well, I said. "You didn't say nothing about no dang pistols or shooting. If that's the way it's going to be, I'd just as soon not get involved."

I was smiling when I said it, so Charlie wouldn't get the idea that I was actually scared or nothing like that, but when you get right down to it, I meant it. I don't figure money is worth all that much if you have to risk getting your head blowed off to get it. I've already been shot at, and it ain't all that much fun.

As soon as we had finished our coffee, we went back to the truck and hauled the paper back down to the pressroom. We had just got it all unloaded and stacked up where Charlie wanted it and was catching our breaths when "Skid" Moore, one of the reporters, came running in from the office side of the newspaper. "There's been a shooting down at the river," he yelled at Charlie.

"We just got a phone call. There's three or four men dead!"

I looked at Charlie and he looked at me, and we both ran for the door.

My truck was right outside, the closest vehicle, so we piled into it and I shot it off down the street and toward the river. From downtown, you drive down Sullivan Street, all the way to the railroad underpass, which is about a mile, before you get to the river. The river is actually closer than that, but the road runs around a couple of fields which make it that far.

13

Just beyond the underpass is where the trouble had happened. The old tannery building is up the river a little way, closer to town, and there is a little island in the river there, not far after you go through the underpass.

The Roller boys old bank building was located on the city side, but they moved it downtown a few years ago and now that building is a grocery store. The front of the building is painted yellow, so it is called the "Yellow Front Market".

On through the underpass, the river runs fairly close to the road. There's an ice house and a few other business buildings along there, and a few little houses that people live in.

The river bank is a kind of park like place.

Folks use it for picnics and fishing and such very often.

We jerked the truck to a stop and jumped out, running over to the edge of the stream to look both directions. I saw some people up the river a little way, and we headed for them at a run.

Halfway there, we came across this teenage boy, who was mad as a wet hen.

"What happened here, boy?" Charlie asked him,

"Blamed so-and-so took my horse," he grumbled. "Just made me get off of him and took him and rode off. He shot them police and then took my horse!"

"Who is shot?" Charlie demanded.

"I don't know," the kid replied. "Some police, I reckon. What am I going to do about my horse? Pa will skin me sure if I don't get him back."

"Oh, damn the horse, boy!" Charlie yelled. "Was any of the officers killed?"

"Oh, all of them, I reckon," the boy said. "Three or four. They're up yonder. I gotta find my horse." Charlie gave an exasperated snort and ran off toward the little knot of people on the riverbank the boy had pointed out. I dogged his heels as fast as I could.

A man was flat on the ground and two others were bending over him.

In a minute, I saw that the man on the ground was John Smith, a city police officer I knew. As I got closer, I could see the blood all over his shirt front and when I noticed how still he was laying there, I knew he had to be dead.

There were four teenage girls and a lanky boy standing in a little bunch over to one side, near some trees. I ran over to them.

14

The lanky boy jerked his head in the direction of down river.

"Over there" he said.

I turned and ran down river for about 60 feet and saw another bunch of men, three of them, kneeling down and working on a man who was sprawled on the ground. They were trying to stuff a handkerchief around a wound in his chest to stem the flow of blood that was gushing out.

When I got close enough, I could see that it was George Frazier, another city policeman I know, who had been shot.

Officer Joe Groseclose was working on him. A man I didn't know, who looked like a farmer and was dressed in overalls, was helping. Deputy George Miller was watching and looking helpless.

I looked over near the bushes at the riverside and saw another body. I could tell it was dead at first glance the man had been shot right through his face, and had taken another bullet in his chest, right through the heart. Blood was all over his face and upper body and I couldn't tell who it might be.

There was nothing I could do there, and I didn't want to get in the way any more than I had to, so I left and went back up to where the girls and lanky boy were bunched up together.

"What happened?" I asked one of them.

"Lord!" she gasped. "They just came running up shooting! We were just standing here talking, and they started shooting at us.

"Kinnie ... it was Kinnie Wagner ... he had a gun and he yelled at us to lay down and he shot back!" She was pale and looked scared.

"I don't know what it was all about. We were just down here to meet him. His sister is here. That's her right over there. She is out of school today and wanted to see him, and we came along... lord!"

I could see that she was crying again, more tears running down the tracks that had already washed traces down both her cheeks.

The girl who had been pointed out as Wagner's sister looked kind of dazed, like she really didn't understand what had happened or what was going on.

I didn't ask any more questions of them, because I could see that it would not do any good, and might just upset them more. I sort of stood back against a tree and watched and listened. Lots of times, you can find out more that way than you can by talking too much.

Wagner's sister had fainted, it seemed, right after the shooting began. There were conflicting stories already, I could tell from just hearing the youngsters talking to each other.

15

Some seemed to think that Wagner had shot first, while others said the police had come running up, shooting at him as they came.

But all of them were agreed on one thing. Kinnie Wagner had pulled out a gun, or maybe two, and stepped behind a tree, and shot back, killing two officers and wounding a third out of the five who had tried to take him. One officer had fallen over and pretended to be dead, lying as still as a rock until Wagner grabbed the boy's horse and rode away before he had shown any sign of life at all. The fifth officer had taken to his heels and ran like a frightened deer away from the horrible scene of blood and death and violence.

I never saw as much confusion as there was right after that. People kept coming down there to see what had happened. They came in cars and trucks, on horseback, and even walking. The crowd was milling around, getting in the way of the officers and even the ambulance fellows who came down to pick up the bodies.

After the dead men had been taken away and the wounded officer delivered to the Riverview Hospital just down the road a piece to be patched up, folks were still coming and standing around looking.

One man came over and stepped behind a tree.

"This is where he shot them from!" he called out to his companions. Then all of them had to come over there and take turns stepping behind the tree and peeking out, as if they were shooting at something over in the field.

The officers had already picked up the spent cartridges but some of the men and boys who were there got to hunting for more, and even old shotgun shells, left over from last winter's squirrel hunting, suddenly took on a new significance, and were quickly gathered up as treasures and souvenirs.

Rocks, shells from down at the river and even leaves were grabbed, as if they were magical pieces of a historical scene that would become family treasures.

I couldn't see much sense to it myself. It seemed kind of silly to be standing around with a bunch of people like that, so when I heard that the officers were organizing a posse to go after the gunman, I sort of let myself get volunteered.

There must have been three dozen or more of us, and we were split up into three groups. One group was to go over toward the Scott County Road, which runs into Virginia past Oak Hill Cemetery and that way; another bunch was to go down river and follow the North Fork, by way of the ford over in Carters Valley. The group I was with were assigned to go up Howard Hill, which runs down almost to the river where the shooting took place, up over Cherry Hill and down the other side, and then comb cross-country toward Virginia from that direction, because that's where the gunman was last seen, or at least the direction he was heading toward when he rode off on the "borrowed" horse. We took off at a fast pace, thinking we might find him some place near town.

There were horse hoof tracks going in that direction alright, and we figured sure we were hot on his trail.

I learned later that at least one witness ... a little boy, scarcely more than a toddler, had actually seen the horseman ride past. That was Scott Pyle's little son, Carl, who was playing outside at the time. There may have been many others, but the Pyle child is the only one I know of who actually saw the escaping gunman ride past.

Our group of the posse was enthused, thinking sure we'd find the killer before darkness set in. We checked smokehouses and barns and all kinds of outbuildings including privies, but we didn't find a trace of the shooter.

There were quite a few guns in our group, and some of the men looked kind of trigger-happy to me, so I tried to stay out of the line of fire in case one of them got a glimpse of a rabbit or something and started blasting away, thinking he was shooting at the desperado. The deputy in charge kept trying to get them into some kind of order, but it didn't do much good. They would veer off at every opportunity to check out any possible hiding place, and they did it in such a way that if the gunman had actually been hiding there, we would probably have some more dead men on our hands, so I was just as glad that we didn't find anyone.

It's a long walk up over that high hill and down to the river on the farside, but we made it before dark, and we were milling around on the riverbank, trying to get the deputy to make up his mind what we were supposed to do next when this other officer came riding up on a horse.

He had been along with the group that went down river and over to the ford, he said, and they had not found any trace of the gunman, so the next thing to do was follow the river into Virginia and cross it where we could, because he figured we were definitely on the shooter's trail now.

They hassled around there for some little time. It seemed like the deputy sheriff who was leading our part of the posse was afraid to take us across the stateline into Virginia until he got a Virginia deputy or sheriff, or somebody who had some authority from our neighboring state, so they could deputize us all over again, for the state of Virginia instead of Tennessee, if that's what it took to make us official.

That took some time to get done.

Our deputy had to send the horse-riding deputy to Gate City, Virginia, to get their sheriff to come over to where we were and re-deputize us when we crossed the state line and went into Virginia.

After it finally got done, it was beginning to get late evening, and night shadows were already creeping in. The sun had set, and twilight settled down quickly.

We crossed the river at the old bridge on the Scott County Road, and then we split up into three groups again, with one heading toward Hiltons, which cuts up a valley toward Bristol; another group going down the Poor Valley Road, which runs nearly to Rogersville; and the bunch I was with headed toward Gate City, Virginia, to see if we could find the gunman.

Kinnie Wagner, the shooter we were searching for, lived near Gate City when he was a youngster. He had a lot of relatives and friends over that way, and we figured there was a mighty good chance he would go there to hide out.

The officers from Kingsport had driven some cars over, so we got to ride the last part of the way, for which I was thankful, because my feet were plumb wore out, not being used to walking so much or so far over rough ground, and uphill most of the way at that.

Going to Gate City from Kingsport you go through Moccasin Gap and then into the little Virginia town. One of the first things you pass is the old Barrel Stave Mill.

They claim it is the biggest barrel stave mill in the world, and it could be for all I know. Some folks call Gate City the "Barrel Stave Capital". There were long rows of lumber stacked up outside the mill, like a sawmill yard, and there were piles of sawdust and scrap that had been discarded, and we checked all through them because they looked like fine hiding places, but there wasn't anyone there.

It was full dark by now, and that old barrel stave yard was a spooky place to be.

One feller who was along, Jess Jones, tripped and knocked over a couple of boards that were propped loosely against a stack, and they fell over with a bang that sounded like a gunshot.

Three or four of the gun-happy posse members threw up their guns and started shooting, not knowing what they were shooting at or where

18

it could be, and the Virginia Deputy Sheriff who was now in charge had a fit. He hollered out and cussed at them and made them stop, and then he lit in on them and gave them a dressing down that smarted some against everybody along, including me, and I hadn't even had a blamed gun.

But after he told them there would be no more shooting unless and until he said so, everybody got kind of meek.

I figured that a lot of the fellers had come along as a sort of a lark, looking for some fun and excitement, and maybe being in on the capture of a desperado they could brag and tell about for years, but it didn't seem to work out that way at all.

We went on to Gate City before our bunch give up and kind of fizzled out. There wasn't any sign of a gunman and nobody we talked to seemed to know anything about it or hadn't seen nothing, and couldn't care less anyways, so we just give up and went back home.

We piled in the cars the Deputies drove and hung on, getting back to Kingsport about 11:00 that night. Nick's was closed, but Shaffer's was still open, and I made a beeline for it to get something to eat and catch up on the news, if any, since I'd been gone.

There was a copy of the evening newspaper on Shaffer's counter, so I picked it up to read.

"TWO LOCAL OFFICERS ARE KILLED BY A DESPERADO" the headlines screamed.

"SMITH AND WEBB ARE DEAD. FRAZIER IS WOUNDED IN RUNNING GUN BATTLE.

I sank down in one of the booths and motioned for the girl behind the counter to bring me over a cup of coffee. She came over with a big, steaming mug, and I ordered a couple of hamburgers.

Then I settled back to wait and read the news, to see if it was like I had seen and heard for myself.

The paper was dated Monday, April 13, 1925.

Down under the big headlines were smaller lines, sort of like the big city newspapers do all the time.

"Fugitive Takes Horse from Man and Makes Escape"

"Posses Are Organized"
"Desperado Comes From Behind Tree and Begins Firing With Two Guns as Officers Approach from Upper Side"

The story finally started, half way down the page.

19

"Deputy Sheriff Hubert Webb and Policeman John Smith were shot to death and Policeman George Frazier was wounded by a desperado, supposed to be a fugitive by the name of Wagner, wanted in Mississippi on a serious charge, in a running gun battle between five officers and the fugitive on the banks of the Holston River just below Old Kingsport underpass at about 4 o'clock this afternoon.

"Both Webb and Smith fell and died in their tracks. One shot penetrated Webb's face just to the left of his nose while another bullet glazed his shoulder and passed through his heart. Either wound would have proven almost instantly fatal.

"Smith was shot directly through his heart, and his death, too, must have been instantaneous.

"Officer Frazier was shot through the left breast, the bullet coming out through the left shoulder blade. This was the only wound which he sustained and while his wound is serious, it is not believed by attending physicians that it will prove fatal.

"He was rushed immediately to the Riverside Hospital where he is now resting easily.

"After shooting the officers, the desperado took a horse from Dewey Nelson at the point of a pistol and, mounting, galloped off through the underpass in the direction of Old Kingsport. He is said to subsequently have been seen riding furiously in the direction of Cherry Hill.

"Other towns and rural districts have been notified by telephone and telegraph of the affair and by 5 o'clock a posse of officers and deputized citizens had been organized and were in pursuit of the fugitive.

"With the whole countryside aroused and the roads, fields and woodlands being scoured in every direction, there was every reason to believe that the fugitive would be apprehended before nightfall.

"The officers in the posse which engaged in the pistol battle with the stranger were Deputy Sheriff Joe Groseclose, Deputy Sheriff Miller, Officer Frazier, and the two men who were killed. "The stranger, who was supposed to have been armed with two heavy .38 caliber pistols, was alone in the fight, but was supposed to have been in a party of three women and one other man just before the battle began.

"The officers had been notified that a group of men and women were by the side of the river at the point where the shooting later occurred and, according to information received at police headquarters, the members of the party were believed to be guilty of indecent conduct.

"The officers, on receiving this information, went immediately to the spot indicated, where they encountered the desperado."

The girl brought my hamburgers over just as I finished the story, and I picked up one of them and took a bite, still scanning over the newspaper page for other information, but that was all it said.

I found out later that the bunch of deputies I had been with was just a little group that got sent over to Gate City just in case the gunman might have gone that way, where his relatives lived, but the main posse had headed over toward Waycross, Virginia, which is where he really was, as was later learned, but they didn't find him.

Our group probably should have gone down there and joined the hunt, but nobody told us to do anything like that, and I was just as glad that the deputy who had been in charge decided he would rather go home and forget it, because I felt the same blamed way myself.

As it turned out, none of that search had been necessary anyhow, because Wagner turned himself in the next morning to a feller named Poe over at Waycross, and we could all have saved ourselves a blamed lot of trouble and a lot of walking and tired feet if we had of known he was going to do that.

Maybe the best way to tell it is to just reprint the following day's newspaper account of it. They sometimes get things messed up, but you can mostly count on part of it being right enough to where you can pretty well understand what really happened, and here's what they printed that day, Tuesday, April 14, 1925:

"GUN DESPERADO SURRENDERS"
"WAGNER LODGED IN BLOUNTVILLE
JAIL, AWAITING HIS TRIAL"

"Kinnie Wagner Gave Himself Up to D.R. Poe at Waycross About 8 O'Clock This Morning

"He said He Thought He Killed Two Men Here Yesterday and Probably Three"

"Was Surrounded by 100 Men Last Night—Was Cheerful"

"Kinnie Wagner, the two-gun man, desperado and fugitive from justice who killed two officers and seriously wounded another here yesterday afternoon in an open gun battle on the banks of the Holston

21

River quietly gave himself up to D.R. Poe at the latter's store near Waycross, Va., at 8:1 0 o'clock this morning.

"Wagner is now lodged in the Blountville jail where he will await a specially arranged trial which will probably come up at this session of the Sullivan County Criminal Court. It was announced late this afternoon that the trial will be held at Blountville on next Tuesday. Three indictments were made against Wagner, two for murder and a third for felonious assault.

"According to Poe's story, Wagner came to the store this morning and when about 30 feet from the porch on which Poe and a number of others were standing, hailed them from this distance and stated that he would like to give himself up, and that he didn't want but one person to come out to meet him.

"Poe stated that none of the other men standing near him on the porch were willing to approach the stranger and that he was the only one to make any move toward the man. He stated that Wagner remarked that he had killed as many as he wanted to and was now ready to surrender without further violence, and was not willing to give up to an officer, and that he would, under no circumstances submit himself into the custody of an officer of the law, but would shoot it out with any number."

"Asked for Protection"

"After giving the gun to Poe and in the presence of five other witnesses on the store porch, Wagner asked that he be taken to an officer and that his companions not allow him to be mobbed, according to the story told by Poe.

"Wagner requested that he be taken to an officer in Gate City. Poe and Neil Bussel, the latter having come along in a Ford Roadster about the time of Wagner's surrender, put Wagner in the roadster and started in the direction of Gate City. Poe stated that he then discovered that Wagner had another gun on his person and when Poe asked for it, he told him that he would give it to him in a little while, Poe said.

"Shortly after this remark, Bussel, Poe and Wagner met Deputy Sheriffs George Clark and Ruben Fulk, accompanied by G. D. Lane at a point about one and a half miles from Moccasin Gap.

"At this point the car in which the officers were driving collided with that of Mr. Bussel and both automobiles were damaged considerably.

22

"None of the men in the cars sustained any serious injuries, however, although some were thrown from the machine."

"Deputy Fulk was shaken up quite a bit but no serious injuries are apparent. Two of the wheels on the officer's car were damaged. They started for Gate City in the Ford Roadster

"But Wagner and Poe came to town with the sheriffs Fulk and Clark. Bussel did not accompany the others to Kingsport.

"Poe stated that the road was narrow at the point where the cars met and that he believed the accident was unavoidable while Deputy Fulk claims that he recognized one of the men in the roadster as Wagner and that he cut into the roadster purposely to check the progress of the smaller automobile.

"Deputy Fulk claims that the three men in the roadster got out of the wreckage and began walking out the road when he remarked to Deputy Clark "that's the man," and the two approached the others and took the other gun off Wagner.

"This was the larger gun, and was the one which Wagner said he did the killing with yesterday, according to Poe, who believed the collision an accident. Wagner told the officers that he had already surrendered to Poe and that had he not already done so, the officers would never have approached him as they did.

"He offered no resistance whatever when he saw the officers, for Poe said he was satisfied with having surrendered to someone other than an officer and did not wish to show any further violence.

"Before Wagner left the store, Poe told that the fugitive was intent on shooting himself but that he, Bussel and others persuaded the desperado to abolish such an idea. Shortly after coming to the store and giving himself up to Poe, Wagner requested that the latter write a letter to his father and one to his sister. Poe complied with the request and wrote the letters at the dictation of the fugitive who stated to his sister that he wanted her to have half the reward which is offered for his capture and that the other half be given to the man to whom he had surrendered. The letter to his father contained practically the same request. The fugitive's father, C.M. Wagner, lives at Speers Ferry, Va., and one sister, Ollie, lives in Kingsport. Another lives in Gate City."

"Surrounded by Posse"

"Wagner told Poe that there were more than 100 men on all sides of him last night but none were within several miles of him this morning.

23

"The fugitive spent the latter part of the night in a barn located on the farm of Mrs. Sam Rhodes, a widow living near Waycross.

"She told Poe that some man had come to her house last night and told her he was in trouble, but she did not state whether he asked for food or shelter. It is probable that he asked for the latter since the fugitive himself said he spent part of the night in a barn.

"The two-gun desperado was in a cheerful mood when brought to police headquarters this morning. When he was put in a car which carried him to the Blountville jail, Wagner was smoking a cigarette and smiling as if nothing whatever had happened to him. He was very quiet and displayed no violent attitude at any time."

"Admits Mississippi Killing"

"Poe stated that Wagner admitted to him of having killed someone in Mississippi and also discussed in part the affair here yesterday.

"Wagner told Poe that he thought he killed two men here yesterday and probably three. He further stated that he had shot three times at one man. This was probably Deputy Sheriff Webb who was the recipient of two bullet wounds, the other officers were shot only once. Further discussion of the shooting yesterday by the desperado revealed that he concealed himself behind a tree when he saw the officers and that he began shooting while there, according to the story told to Poe.

"Wagner stated that he shot one man while concealed behind the tree and then turned in the opposite direction and shot another. After this he told Poe he stepped out in the open and shot his way through.

"Poe stated that the desperado did not talk very much more about the shooting here yesterday, but that he willingly entered into conversation on most any topic. He told Poe that after making his escape from the scene of the shooting yesterday he rode the horse which he took from Dewey Nelson until he crossed the North Fork River, after which he started the animal down the river, and he proceeded in the opposite direction.

"Wagner said he did not cross the river at any regular fording place, but rode across at the point he came to the water.

"The daring gunman was barefooted this morning.

"He told Poe that he swam Possum Creek last night leaving his shoes on the other side. His clothing was damp and he was suffering from chills when he surrendered to Poe, who loaned him a sweater.

24

"Poe said that Wagner gave the gun to him, and requested that he keep it and that the other gun which he intended to give to Poe be given to his father."

"The .32 Smith & Wesson revolver which the desperado gave to Poe was loaded. Wagner had two holsters belted about his waist. His other gun was a .38 caliber Special. Poe told that one man who was about the store when the desperado made his appearance took to his heels and that Wagner laughingly asked if the man was an officer, later remarking that "that was the way officers usually did" when they saw him.

"However the man was not an officer, Poe stated.

"The reports that Wagner was wearing steel shield-plates proved erroneous since no plates of any kind were revealed on his person this morning. He was not touched by a bullet during the battle yesterday."

"Traveled With Circus"

"Wagner is said to have traveled with a circus for some time during which time he was employed as an expert pistol artist.

"He proved to be an excellent shot yesterday having hit all three of the officers near the heart.

"More than 100 men and officers scoured the country last night in an effort to apprehend the daring desperado but to no avail.

"Bloodhounds were secured from Pulaski and put on the trail where the horse was found exhausted, but the hounds were of little value in the search. After the horse was found near Clouds Ford the posse trailed the fugitive to a piece of woodland near Waycross, where they thought they had him surrounded, and probably did, but he slipped through at a later hour in the night, and after a thorough search of the woods had been made the posse sought the desperado in another direction.

"The dead and injured officers were members of a party of five sent to search for a party of men and women on the Holston River who were reportedly guilty of disorderly conduct. The officers were taken by surprise when Wagner opened fire on them, which brought death to two of the party and wounded another."

"Frazier Doing Nicely"

"Policeman Frazier is reported to be doing nicely and there are hopes for his recovery.

"Funeral services for Policeman John Smith were held this afternoon. Deputy Sheriff H. D. Webb will be buried here tomorrow."

"POLICEMAN JOHN SMITH BURIED AT PYLES CEMETERY
—Services were in charge of Lovelace L.O.O.F"
"Was Faithful Member of Police Force"
"Funeral services for Policeman John Smith, one of the victims of the shooting affray here yesterday afternoon, were conducted this afternoon at 3 o'clock followed by internment in Pyles Cemetery. "Services were in charge of the local order of L.O.O.F."

"Mr. Smith had been a member of the city police force for several months and during that time has been a faithful officer to the cause. He was 38 years old.

"Mr. Smith is survived by his father and mother, Mr. and Mrs. C. L. Smith of near here, one sister, Mrs. Maude Ketron, and one brother, Ernest Smith of Kingsport.

"He is also survived by his wife and 6 children, 3 girls, Lee May, Irene and Hazel, and 3 boys, Roy, William and John Jr. Mr. Smith has been a member of the Odd Fellows for sometime.

"Funeral Services for Deputy H.D. Webb will be held tomorrow afternoon followed by internment in the City Cemetery."

"FUNERAL SERVICE FOR H. D. WEBB WILL BE HELD TOMORROW SERVICES WILL BE CONDUCTED FROM FIRST CHRISTIAN CHURCH BY REV WALKER.
"Internment in City Cemetery"
"Funeral Services for Deputy Sheriff Hubert D. Webb, who was shot to death here yesterday afternoon by Kinnie Wagner, desperado and fugitive from justice, will be conducted at the First Christian Church at 2 o'clock tomorrow afternoon, it was announced today by his brother, H. C. Webb.

"Rev. William P Walker, pastor of the church, will officiate.

"The services at the church will be followed by internment in the City Cemetery. It was announced that pallbearers will be Cham A. King, H.K. Starnes, J.H. Parrott, B.H. Russell, Joe Groseclose, and W. W. Leedy, all of whom are either deputy sheriffs of Sullivan County or members of the Kingsport Police Force.

"Flower bearers will be chosen from Shelborne Ferguson's Sunday School Class of the First Christian Church. Deputy Sheriff Webb was a member of the Christian Church and was 25 years old.

"He is survived by his wife and three children.

"He also leaves 4 brothers, H.C., Fred, and Woodrow of Kingsport and V. G. of Goldsboro, N.C., and his father and mother, Mr. and Mrs. D. H.Webb of Kingsport."

As you can guess, the shoot out and Kinnie Wagner's surrender were all the talk that day, just about anywhere you went. The newspaper ran a letter from the sheriff in Mississippi with a description of Wagner in it, and from that, everybody you talked to knew all about him, had known him all his life, and was a close friend of his, unless they happened to be one of the few folks who were siding with the police, of which there were some of, and most of them fairly important folks, too.

Here's what the description letter said, reprinted from the newspaper:

"DESCRIPTION OF A TWO GUN DESPERADO"

"...following is a detailed description of Kinnie Wagner, the daring desperado who is now lodged in the Blountville jail, issued by W. J. Turner, Sheriff of Greene County, Mississippi, where Wagner is wanted for the murder of a deputy sheriff:

"I will pay $1,000 for Kinnie Wagner, alias Tully Wagner, dead or alive, who shot and killed M. M. McIntosh, Deputy Sheriff of Greene County Mississippi, on the twenty-fourth day of December, 1924.

"Wagner is a young white man, about 26 years of age, six feet tall, weight 170 pounds, has black, coarse, wavy hair and brown eyes, has well-developed shoulders and chest, hips and lower extremities not too well developed.

"It is claimed that this man has several scars on his body caused from bullet wounds, one of which is said to be though the side just about the hip and another through the inside of one hip, close up to the crotch and another said to be through the shoulder.

"He is also said to have a scar or indenture in the chest, caused by the horn of a saddle, but I cannot be positive as to any of these scars.

"Wagner came to this country from Texas as a bronco buster with a so-called Wild West Show about 3 years ago, and frequently puts on the appearance and plays the role of a cowboy.

"He is an expert marksman with a gun and pistol and usually goes heavily armed and frequently plays the game of "hold up man" especially among the Negroes.

"It is said that he is wanted somewhere in Texas for murder.

"Write or wire me for any further information or further description."

There was a lot of other things going on in the world that day, too, but they didn't make much notice in Kingsport.

Down in Jellico, Tennessee, the chief of police, Tom Baldwin, was shot to death by a drunken negro, who had been creating a disturbance by shooting at cars as they passed. The black, named Jim Edwards, had his body riddled with bullets of a posse, led by Deputy Sheriff James Bowlin, who apparently started shooting as soon as they got him in their sights.

The Associated Press story told how the police were armed only with shotguns and two revolvers, while the negro had a big revolver and a high-powered rifle, and had taken cover behind a tree.

Over in Bristol, Tennessee-Virginia, just twenty miles or so to the North and East from Kingsport, police and angry citizens were conducting a bush-to-bush search to find a negro there who was reported to have assaulted an 11 year old school girl a few hours earlier.

I had just finished breakfast that morning and was getting ready to go hunt up some hauling business when some come up and found me.

Irwin Fuller come in and said he had been looking for me, on account of he had bought some office furniture at an auction sale over in Bristol, and he wanted me to go over there and load it up and haul it back for him.

That was just the sort of job I was planning to look for, so we settled on a price and he gave the address where I should pick it up and a list of what I was to get and I got out the truck and lit out for Bristol.

By the time I got to Blountville, I met a car loaded with armed men and deputies. They had rifles and shotguns sticking out of the windows there was so many of them, and it looked like they were off to fight a war, or start one, or something. They didn't even look in my direction as they passed, which kind of puzzled me some.

I figured that maybe they didn't know that Kinnie Wagner had surrendered and they were going over to Kingsport to help hunt for him, and I would have told them that he was already in jail if they had of given me a chance to do it, but they didn't so I didn't either, and I just drove on toward Bristol and ignored it as best I could.

But in a little while, I met another car loaded up with armed men the same way, and then another!

When I got to the outskirts of Bristol, there were armed men on foot, with guns and clubs and even pitchforks, looking under every rock and behind every bush!

I stopped the truck and asked one gang of men what on earth was going on and they told me that this Negro man had attacked a little 11year old girl there in Bristol, and they were going to find him.

It was pretty obvious what they had in mind to do with the man if and when they did find him, too, but I didn't say nothing about that. A man that attacks any 11-year-old girl kind of needs the sort of attention they had in mind for a cure, no matter what color his skin may be, I figure.

I pieced the story together finally and got it sort of straight in my mind.

Little Thelma McCrary, an 11-year-old schoolgirl, had got the idea into her head somehow that because last Sunday was Easter, there would not be any school the next day. And in the same way an eleven year old gets that kind of idea all twisted up in her mind, she also thought that there was to be an Easter Egg Hunt at the school right after lunch.

And so, being a normal school girl, she did what any other 11 year old would do and slept late that day. Then, after lunch, she lit out for the school, skipping merrily along toward the school yard, only to find out that she was a half day late for school, and had already missed arithmetic class and spelling, and was now late for Geography.

Thelma didn't have her Geography book, naturally, and the teacher told her to run home and get it right away, because she would need it for the class.

On her way home, the girl passed by a large boulder at the side of the road. A black man, she said, stepped out from behind the boulder and told her that someone wanted to see her up on the ridge.

Thelma was frightened and tried to run, but the black man pulled out a big revolver and stuck it against her chest and told her not to scream. One of his hands clamped down on her shoulder, she said, and she struggled to get loose, but the black man choked her and tore her dress from around her shoulders.

But then, the little girl broke loose and ran away, meeting a man further down the street, to whom she told her story. He took her to a nearby filling station and there telephoned for the police.

Before you could unhitch a team, there was a mob of men and police involved in the search for the black man. They got bloodhounds and put them on the trail. Every available policeman in Bristol showed up and more than 100 men volunteered as deputies. The hunt was, I guess actually bigger than the search for Kinnie Wagner had been over in Kingsport, and the posse was a heck of a lot madder than the bunch looking for the shooting "desperado" had been.

I figured if they ever caught that black guy, they'd string him up for sure, without asking any questions or bothering with a trial, and when I saw a coil of rope here and there in the crowd, looped around some "deputy's" shoulder, I knew blamed well that is just what they had in mind.

Well, I went on down into Bristol and got the load of furniture and office stuff that Irvin had sent me over there for, and there were people talking everywhere about the negro's attack on the little girl.

It was blamed near as much as the Kinnie Wagner shootout talk had been over at home.

If anything, people in Bristol were even more excited, and most of them were plain mad about it. The shootout had been bad enough, I reckon, and I know that the families of the men who were killed were mad, and so were their friends, but over here, danged near everybody was angry over this thing.

They arrested a negro man down in Blountville and hauled him back to Bristol for the girl to look at, but she said he wasn't the one who had bothered her and they had to let him go. Then they got another black man over in Bluff City, and went through that same thing all over again, but he still wasn't the man who done what he done, the little girl said.

They didn't know the black man's name they were looking for, they didn't know where he lived or what he looked like, exactly, or nothing else at all about him, except that the little girl said he had attacked her near the Old Mill Wood Property that afternoon, and they had been hunting for him ever since.

She had given the police a good description of her assailant, but the fact that he was a black man was the main thing that stuck out in people's minds, and they made every black man they happened to see a suspect.

I bought a copy of the Bristol Herald Courier and read about it. The newspaper said officers N.E. Trainman, Clarence Manis, W. J. Rogers and Bed Odell had spent the entire night looking for the Negro suspect, and had helped organize the posse of more than 100 volunteers.

Cars of armed men were running around on every street you came to. They didn't know which way the suspect had gone, if he had, and had no idea of where he might be, so a careful canvas of practically every street in West and South Bristol had been made, but with no favorable results, at least for the searchers.   The posse even sent a large group of men out and searched the knob-like hill at the southwest end of town, but they didn't find the suspect or anyone who had seen him or knew anything about him.

I don't think they ever found him, but I don't know for sure. Personally, I got out of there as soon as I could. When there are that many angry men with that many guns, anything can happen, and I had experienced enough excitement for two short days.

But about halfway to Blountville, I got to worrying some about what if that black guy had seen my truck, loaded up like it was and covered over with a tied-down tarpaulin in case of unexpected rain, and climbed in and hid among the office furniture.

So I stopped along the side of the road and got out and checked all through the load, but there wasn't nothing in the truck but what was supposed to be there.

I got back on my way, feeling a little silly, but mighty well relieved.

It would be bad enough to be the negro they were hunting, if they caught up with him, but I blamed sure wouldn't want to be the feller who got caught helping him get away, even if it wasn't intentional because you didn't even know he was there.

I thought about stopping at the Blountville jail to see if I could get a look at Wagner, now that he was locked up, or see if I could find out any more about that all, but I considered it some and decided I had better sense, and I just headed back to Kingsport as fast as I could get away with driving in a loaded down old truck like mine.

The following day the Times, our local newspaper, was back on the Kinnie Wagner story again. The headlines screamed:

"KINNIE WAGNER REMAINS IN CHEERFUL MOOD"

"Youthful Gunman and Desperado to be Tried Tuesday Spends Night Under Heavy Guard in Blountville Jail.

"No Violence Shows.

"Conflicting Tales of Capture Related.

"Wagner Admits Having Shot Deputy Sheriff in Mississippi

"Says He Fired Five Shots Here Monday"

"Kinnie Wagner, desperado and confessed slayer of two officers here Monday afternoon, seemed to be in the same cheerful spirit today after spending last night under heavy guard in the Blountville jail where he was placed yesterday morning after having surrendered to D. R. Poe, a general merchant at Waycross, Tenn." I noticed that Waycross, Tenn," which should really have been Waycross, Virginia, but the local paper is always making little mistakes like that, and nobody pays much attention to it, on account of they are used to it. You have to read what they mean, sometimes, not what they write, you see.

"The Sullivan County Grand Jury was in session yesterday and immediately considered Wagner's case when he was taken to Blountville yesterday morning, and returned three indictments against him, two for murder and a third for felonious assault.

"Wagner will be placed on trial next Tuesday, Judge Guy S. Chase appointed general counsel for the defense and set the date for the trial.

"George M. Warren and Lyle Burrow, both of Bristol, will act as counsel for the defendant while Attorney General O. B. Lovette, of Greeneville, will represent the prosecution. He will be assisted by T.R. Bandy, City Attorney, and also a number of local lawyers who are given the opportunity of assisting in the case if they so desire.

"Attorney General Lovette requested that they be given the opportunity to volunteer their services.

"Conflicting Stories Related"
"Conflicting tales are being related about the capture of Wagner yesterday morning. His being lodged in the jail yesterday morning brought to close one of the most exciting and daring manhunts that this section has experienced in many years.

"Posses were formed here immediately after the shooting Monday afternoon, and the search was still in progress yesterday morning when the fugitive gave himself up at Poe's store.

"According to the story told yesterday by Poe, Wagner came to the store and while some little distance away, hailed him and others who were standing on or near the store porch, and asked that one man come out to meet him, because he wanted to give himself up.

"Poe stated that no one but himself made any attempt to approach the man, and that Wagner asked him if he had any guns before he approached the fugitive. He afterwards came to the store and had Poe write the letters to his father and sister.

"Poe also stated that Wagner wanted to commit suicide but that he and others at the store persuaded him not to carry out his intention.

"He consented to be taken to Gate City to officers, but requested that Poe and Neal Bussel, who came along in a Ford roadster in which the three men started to Gate City, not allow anyone to mob him.

"While on their way to Gate City they met Deputy Sheriff George Clark and Ruben Fulk, accompanied by G.D. Lane.

"Sheriff Fulk claims that he recognized Wagner and ran into the Ford Roadster in an effort to affect a capture."

Poe had said it was an accident that the cars bumped into each other. Fulk said he did it deliberately to capture Wagner. Somebody was lying.

I had a hunch that a lot more lies were going to be told before this thing was all over.

The stories were flying around more than ever by now. One tale had it that the police had heard about the $1,000 reward for Wagner, dead or alive, and they figured to get him quick and split the money five ways, making $200 each for a quick and easy job.

Some said the police got out of their car with their guns already drawn and ready to shoot, and that they started shooting as soon as they saw Wagner and the other people there on the riverbank.

Others claimed that Wagner started shooting first, when he looked up and saw the officers coming toward him.

The legends about Wagner's powers with a gun grew like nothing I had ever heard of before.

It was said that he pulled his guns out, both of them, quick-draw style like Tom Mix, twirled them a few times around his forefinger, then calmly shot the officers down in cold blood.

Another story had it that he shot one of the officers, and, just to prove he could do it, turned his back toward the other one and pulled out a mirror from his pocket and held it up so he could see behind himself in it, and shot the other officer by pointing his gun backwards, over his shoulder, while he aimed through the looking glass!

A lot of it sounded like nonsense, but I wasn't there when it happened, and I don't know. I didn't see the actual shooting, like I told before, but I was in the first car that got down there after it happened, even if it was a truck. Everybody you met seemed to know something new about how it happened, or some other detail that never got out until they told it.

33

I happened to have some business over on Five Points, which is the busiest, oldest part of town, so I went on over there to take care of it.

There was a little bunch of people gathered around outside the Sullivan Street Cafe, and they seemed to be excited over something.

I walked over to see what was going on and they said that the woman who lived upstairs had just come down the steps with her throat cut from ear to ear.

There was a doctor who just happened to be over at the drugstore across the street when it happened, they said, and he was back in the kitchen of the cafe right at that minute, trying to dress the wound and stop it from bleeding to maybe save her life.

I looked inside at the stair steps and there was a trail of blood running all the way up them, sure enough.

I knew a feller who lived in an apartment up there. He worked parttime at the restaurant there, and sometimes he worked at the lunch stand they have out there at the new Borden Mills Cotton Mill. John some-thing-or-other, his name was. I tried to remember it.

Irrick. That was it.

John Irrick.

He was a quiet kind of man, and seldom had anything to say, but he seemed like a likeable enough sort of chap.

"Who did it, do you know?" I asked one of the people standing around there on the sidewalk. "She said it was her husband" a woman said. "John Irrick is his name."

Well, the long and short of it was that they had been having what is usually called "family troubles" and John apparently decided to try to solve it all with a butcher knife.

That afternoon, the local newspaper's front page was so filled with gore and screams about the throat-cutting, the Kinnie Wagner shoot-out story even got crowded off.

The Trial of Kinnie Wagner

What happened when Kate Irrick staggered down the stairs with her throat cut and they called the law, was a kind of Kingsport classic, I thought. Deputy Sheriff John Parrott was the first officer to reach the scene after it was reported to the police headquarters.

He found that Dr. B. E. Marsh had run over from the drug store where he had stopped to get some prescriptions filled, and had temporarily dressed the gash-like wound so the woman could be transported to Riverview Hospital, where stitches might be taken, not waiting for the ambulance.

Parrott jumped in his car and drove out Sullivan, turning off at the first left corner and taking a right into Dale. He followed Dale Street out toward Horse Creek Road, because he knew that Irrick frequently walked out that way to go to the Borden plant for his job at the lunchstand.

Sure enough, there was John Irrick, calmly walking along, heading toward Horse Creek Road. He stopped when Parrott hailed him, and offered no objection or violence when the officer placed him under arrest.

Parrott asked him why he cut his wife's throat.

Irrick replied: "You know I don't talk much, John. It was over family trouble and you know women will get you into trouble."

That's all he said, or would say, about it, being a man of few words. I wondered if that was part of the trouble between him and his wife. He talked so little that she probably talked too much, like many women do, and he must of got tired of listening to it and decided to shut if off for good and all.

They hauled John Irrick off to the Blountville jail, to stand trial for attempted murder. The folks on the sidewalk milled around for a while and talked about it some more. They had known both the Irrick woman and her husband, and were surprised at the incident, they said.

Her sister had gone to the hospital with Mrs. Irrick, and she called back up to the cafe to say that Mrs. Irrick was going to live, the doctors thought, and may completely recover. That kicked off another round of talk about it, but it soon fizzled out, so I left and went on home. The talk of the throat-cutting family squabble of the Irricks died down by the next day, and folks were already back to talking about the coming trial of Kinnie Wagner. The paper had another lead story in it that day, and at least a small part of it was new.

"Kinnie Wagner remains undisturbed in the Blountville jail, awaiting the trial for his life which is scheduled for Tuesday," it said.

"The youthful desperado will face the court on three charges, two for murder and a third for a felonious assault. It is not yet definitely known who will assist Attorney General O. B. Lovett with the prosecution, but a number of local lawyers will probably enter into the case.

"T. R. Bandy, City Attorney will assist the attorney general, and it has been announced that Worley and McAmis of this city will also assist with the prosecution. Others have been contemplating the matter, but have not yet reached any decision."

Well, that figured. Some of our local lawyers figured that it was good business to be involved in the prosecution, and some of the others figured it would be better business to stay out of it, because the people in town seemed to be split over how they felt about it. In fact, most of the folks I talked to about it seemed to sort of feel that Wagner had done just what he had to do, and what they would have done, if they could have shot that good, and if the situation had got itself forced on them as they thought it got forced on him; but others felt the opposite way, and defended the police and deputies who, they said, had just been doing their jobs.

Everybody around seemed like they claimed to know for certain, one way or another. The trouble I had was trying to figure out how so many people could know things for sure that were just exactly opposite than what some others knowed for certain.

A certain dentist in town had really been shooting his mouth off, I heard, about low-down killers and such, and making big threats about what he would like to do if he had the chance.

But it got out about the reward of $1,000, dead or alive, and pretty well established that the officers knew about that, whether they admitted it or not, and I remembered John Smith asking me if I knowed anything about Wagner's whereabouts, and it did make me sort of doubt the story that they had just kind of gone down there to investigate a complaint of disorderly conduct. Five men with guns seemed like a sort of overdose of peacekeeping, to my mind.

Then there got to be some stories going around about that trouble Wagner got into down in Mississippi that sounded mighty suspicious themselves. According to the newspaper, Wagner had murdered a deputy sheriff named MacIntosh on Christmas Eve. It was said that the deputy had tried to arrest Wagner for stealing a watch.

But the story being told around here was that MacIntosh was a deputy, all right, but also a moonshiner and bootlegger, and what had really happened was that he challenged Wagner to a shooting match, with the watch as a prize, and Wagner beat him. So then MacIntosh claimed the watch was stolen, and went in, gun drawn, shooting at Wagner to try and kill him to get his watch back, and Wagner gunned him down in self-defense.

It was getting more confused every day, and I began to wonder if anybody would ever learn the real truth. One of the things that made the Wagner story even more confusing was the conflicting tales that were being told. At first it was said that he had surrendered.

Then two deputies claimed they had captured him. I figured out that somebody was lying, but it was hard to tell just which bunch it was.

Even the newspaper got kind of exasperated over it.

"Conflicting Tales About Desperado Still Circulating," they said.

"Still the conflicting tales about the capture or surrender of Wagner are being circulated. Deputy Sheriffs Clark and Fulk claim they had placed the desperado under arrest, while D. R. Poe, merchant at the Waycross, says that Wagner gave himself up to him at his store early Tuesday morning."

I guess they forgot that about six or eight other men were with Poe when Wagner surrendered, and nobody supported the deputies' claim but the two of them, but they didn't mention that.

"An interview with Poe yesterday revealed more details of the shooting here Monday afternoon and of Wagner's escape as told to Poe by the fugitive. In his discussion of the affair with Poe, the gunman told of how his trained eye brought two men to the ground at the first shot. He had also told Poe that he was surprised to see the man in civilian clothes standing after he had fired the first shot.

"Hesitating for a few minutes, the gunman told Poe that while he was sure he hadn't missed, he fired the second shot which brought the man in civilian clothes to the ground."

There wasn't nothing mentioned about it, but the word was all over town that Deputy Sheriff Joe Groseclose had ruined a good pair of pants when the shots were fired at him.

I don't know if there was anything to all that or not, and the charge was made that Groseclose had fallen over and played dead until the shooting stopped, which I don't know about either, but which seemed like a purty blamed good idea to me, at any rate. If somebody who could shoot that good was taking shots at me, I reckon I would have a great urge to lay down and play possum, too.

"The daring gunman and ex pistol artist of the circus placed so much confidence in his shooting ability that he never expected to miss," the newspaper story said.

"He also told Poe on their way to Gate City that the reason he did not give him his other gun was because of his fear of being mobbed, and that if he should happen to meet a posse intent on his capture that he would shoot himself rather than be subjected to a mobbing.

"Poe stated that the desperado spoke with all sincerity when talking of his desire to surrender because he 'had killed all he wanted to kill' and that he was ready to be taken to an officer, but had previously decided that he would not be taken by an officer.

"In discussing his adventures Monday night, the fugitive told Poe that he was completely surrounded, but would have shot his way out had it not been for his fear of killing some innocent civilian who was in the searching party. That, he said, was the reason he remained quiet and decided to give himself up before he killed someone that was not a real officer seeking his capture."

"Wagner claims that he shot the officers here Monday because he thought that they were after him and because he was not to be taken alive."

"After having told Poe to write the letters to his father and sister the gunman suggested committing suicide and told Poe to turn his body over to the authorities and instruct them to send it back to Mississippi, for, he said, 'the reward calls for my body, dead or alive.

It had begun to sound to me like that reward business was more vengeance than for justice, and there was more folks thinking that same way.....

There was a dance and a kind of party that night, and I took Molly Mims. I didn't get to see her home, though, and that was a part of a near calamity that could have messed me up good. What happened was that Molly and I had been dancing, and she had been great to dance with and all, and we had just got settled at a table and were laughing and talking and having a fine time when Bill Weems and Mattie Martin showed up.

Mattie is a pretty enough girl, but kind of cold-eyed, with a strict and stern attitude toward life and everything about it. She is a school teacher and looks it. On top of that, she teaches Sunday School, and she acts that, too. Only she acts like she is a teacher for the old folks and very serious about it, seldom smiles, and takes every thing seriously and literally. She is just not a whole lot of fun to be with.

I was kind of surprised to see her at a dance and party with anyone, even though Bill Weems would be about as dull as she was, so they might hit it off fine.

We sat and talked a while, and had a Coke, and Bill asked Miss Mattie to dance, and she said she didn't want to, so he asked me if he could ask Mollie and I told him he'd have to ask her and he did and she did, so they did.

While they were on the dance floor, I struggled along, trying to have a conversation with Miss Mattie, which wasn't the easiest thing in the world to do.

I talked about the weather, and tried to talk about Babe Ruth's operation that he was going to have, but she just muttered yes and no here and there and stared right into my eyes like she was trying to see if there was a speck or a mote in one of them, and she corrected me on my English a couple of times, which I would have appreciated now while I am trying to write this yarn down, but which at the time I didn't care nothing at all about to tell the truth.

I was getting kind of tired of all the talk about Kinnie Wagner, but I even tried some of that. She was interested some, and perked up a bit when we got to the part about the shootings and killings, and she discussed the officer's wounds in some details, and where they were and how bad they had been and how quickly they caused death and all like that, but she didn't have a whole lot of interest in the escape and capture and that part of the story.

I was running out of things to talk about fast. Miss Mattie is a preacher's daughter, and acts like a preacher's wife. She makes scandals out of things very easily, I have been told, and gets offended both quickly and easily.

Then I thought of the Irricks' trouble, and about John cutting his wife's throat like that, and it gave me something else to talk about.

I never could figure out why people get married in the first place if they was going to fight like cats and dogs the rest of their lives, or try to kill each other and all, and Miss Mattie, being a preacher's daughter and a teacher and all might be able to shed some light on why humans act like they do. So I asked her about it. "Miss Mattie", I asked, "what do you think about marriage?"

She stared right into my eyes for the longest time with that serious and grim look of hers.

"Why, yes, Mister Potter," she said. "Yes, I will marry you."

Well, I was what you might call flabbergasted!

Here I had got myself into a mess without doing a blamed thing wrong, so far as I could tell, but just by asking a simple conversational question!

I thought she was funning me for a moment there, but after I took another look at that serious face, with the serious mouth that kind of turned down a little bit at the corners, and those serious eyes that looked as cold as a plate of left-over kraut. I knowed blamed well she wasn't funning about nothing.

"Now, wait a minute," I said.

"I didn't ask you to marry me. I just asked what you thought about marriage, which is a whole different thing!"

After all, I had come to the dance with Molly Mims, and she had come with old Bill Weems, and the only reason at all that I was there at the table with Mattie Martin in the first place was because I had been fool enough to let Bill take Molly out on the dance floor and leave me unprotected.

"Why, Mr. Potter," said Mattie Martin, "are you trying to deny that you asked me to marry you?"

"You are might well told I am," I told her. "One woman getting her throat cut at a time is enough, so you just get that nonsense out of your head."

She sulked about it for the rest of the evening, I'd say, but she didn't have any more to say on the subject.

As soon as Bill and Molly came back to the table, I grabbed Molly's arm and got her out of there as fast as I could, before Mattie could open up her blamed mouth and jump on another confusion.

I got to thinking about it, and I was a little bit worried about old Bill Weems. If Mattie had made up her mind to get married to somebody, she was going to catch some man tonight for sure, and he was the most subjectable, being the one who was with her and all, but that wasn't skin off my nose I reckoned.

I knew a feller who got trapped like that one time, and he was just too blamed polite to get himself off the hook by coming out plain and flat denying that he had meant what the gal claimed he had meant, and they lived unhappily for forty years after that, and I sure wasn't going to let myself be no gentleman if that was what it took to do it.

We went out to my car and started to get in when this smart alec in a yellow Buick drove past and blew his horn. He cut right in close to me as he drove past, and Molly was kind of forced to jump back against me to keep from getting hit. To make it worse, he splashed right through a puddle in the parking area, and got some mud all over both of us.

I had to send Molly on home in Tag Seal's taxi, but Smiddy wasn't driving, so it was alright.

My car was parked a little further down the row, and the big wrench was still under the front seat where I keep it, but by the time I got there, that blamed yellow Buick was already long gone, so I had to just mark it down on my mental note pad to do something about it when the first chance rolled around.

The next day was Sunday, so I slept later than usual. It must have been well after 7 o'clock before I got up, and everybody in the boarding house was still sound asleep then.

I went down the hall to the bathroom and shaved and then run the tub full of hot water and soaked a while. That's one of the nice things about our landlady. She always builds a hot fire in the waterheater stove on Saturday nights in case somebody wants to take a bath early on Sunday. On Saturdays, they have to keep the fire going for the water heater all day long, and the hot water gets used up about as fast as it gets heated. But me and Ted Smith got the bright idea of wrapping some old cow hides and such around the hot water tank, after we put asbestos paper around it, and kind of puffing an extra skin on the outside, and it holds the heat in the water all night long.

Most of the boarders haven't found out about it yet. They get up and shave, and have plenty of hot water for that, and because most of them have already taken their weekly baths on Saturday, they don't bother the full tank, and Ted and I sort of have it all to ourselves, so long as we get to it first, which I usually do. Sunday breakfast is always later than on other days, because the landlady says she needs to get an extra hour sleep herself now and again, so breakfast is not until 9 o'clock, instead of 6 like it is on other days.

I was up and shaved and bathed and dressed long before that, and nobody else had even rolled over the first time, so I went out to the porch and got the Sunday papers. There was the Bristol Herald, which is the big paper, and has all the news in it, and also the Times, which is what passes for a paper here in town, except when the press breaks down.

41

I picked up both of them and sat down in an easy chair beside the parlor window to read.

Both papers had the same picture of Kinnie Wagner on their front pages. He was a tall-looking young man, and in the photograph he was standing against a brick wall, sort of leaning his shoulder back against it. He didn't look like what I thought a killer ought to look like; he was kind of faintly smiling, and looked relaxed and as carefree as you please. I couldn't tell from the picture, but it looked like he was wearing work pants and a plaid shirt, and the shirt was open at the neck to give his neck plenty of air.

"Wagner Trial Set for Tuesday," the headlines said.

We had pancakes for breakfast that Sunday morning, and I guess the strain of the past few days was beginning to tell on me somewhat, because I only ate about four, instead of my usual six.

After breakfast, I went down to the garage I rented and got out my car and drove over to the creek on Dale Street to wash it.

It is a real good place to wash your car. Right after you come through the railroad underpass, if you are coming into town from the direction of Horse Creek, you turn off to the right instead of going on down Sullivan Street, and the road runs right through the shallow branch, which kind of spreads out there, and gives you plenty of room to park right in the water, about 6 to 8 inches deep, so you can scoop up buckets full and pour it right over your car, and it works real fine.

There is not a whole lot of traffic along there on Sunday mornings, at least before 10 a.m., and you can really get into the task at hand. After 10, folks start coming along, going on their way to Sunday school and church, and some of them are in cars, and they splash water all over you if you are still there, so I finished and got out of there before they start coming.

Sometimes I get back home and dress up after I get done and go to church. Not any particular one. I just kind of pick them at random, you might say, or rotate among them, because I never have found one that seems just right somehow. All of them have advantages, I guess, the chief one being that a good many attractive women seem to always be there, but that can sometimes lead to problems of another kind.

On that particular Sunday morning, however, I figured that the preachers would all be worked up over the shootings earlier in the week, and that's what all of them would be talking about and preaching about, and I had heard enough to do me through the day on that subject.

But sometimes things just seem to follow you around, and try though I may, I couldn't get away from the topic. Everywhere I went, folks were discussing it, offering opinions on it, explaining it, until I got plumb tired of hearing about it.

Before the day was over, I had come to the conclusion that if they was going to put Kinnie Wagner on trial Tuesday, I was going to be there and hear it in person, for I was getting blamed tired of everybody telling me something different every time the story got brought up.

Monday's paper was full of news about the coming trial. A venire of 150 to 200 men had been called, it said, from which to select a jury.

"Kinnie Wagner, youthful desperado and confessed slayer of two officers here last Monday afternoon and also confessed murderer of Deputy Sheriff M. M. MacIntosh in Greene County, Mississippi, on last Christmas Eve, will face trial for his life at Blountville next Tuesday. He has been confined in Blountville jail since last Tuesday morning, where he has remained in a cheerful mood and has seemed anxious for his trial to be concluded."

"The Wagner trial will be first of the court's program Tuesday morning. The jury commission was called Friday for the purpose of selecting a venire which will be composed of 150 to 200 men, and these men have now been summonsed or will have been summonsed in time to appear at Blountville when the court convenes Tuesday morning."

"It is probable that the entire first day of the trial will be consumed on the jury, but as soon as the jury is impaneled the trial will begin. All of the states' witnesses have been summonsed to appear at the convening of the session of the criminal court."

"Judge Guy S. Chase of the criminal court of Blountville has appointed George M. Warren and Lyle Burrow, both of Bristol, to represent the defendant, while Attorney General O. B. Lovette of Greeneville, T. R. Bandy and Worley and McAmis, all of Kingsport, will represent the prosecution."

"It is probable that C. T. Herndon and other local lawyers will assist in the case although none other than those ones mentioned here have yet made known their desire to participate in the trial".

Who Gets Reward?

Leaksville, Mississippi, April 18 - if the Tennessee authorities do not turn Kinnie Wagner over to Sheriff W. J. Turner here and permit the man to stand trial in Greene County the chances are they will receive none of the reward offered for the man's capture, dead or alive.

"It was learned here today that Tennessee officers may place Wagner on trial there, and if he is convicted of first degree murder and is executed, turn his body over to Sheriff Turner and make an effort to collect the thousand dollar reward. Just exactly what will happen in connection with this remains to be seen.

"Turner, it is known, has already conferred with the County Attorney here regarding the answer to be given the Tennessee officers in the event they attempt to collect the reward. What decision was reached has not been made known. The thousand dollar award is offered in private subscriptions contributed by friends of Murdock MacIntosh, for whose murder the ex-cow-puncher is wanted here. Dimes and dollars poured in from every section of Greene County and adjoining counties where the MacIntosh family is so well known and so well liked."

"If Tennessee will send Wagner back to Leaksville for trial, the arresting officers will be given the $1,000. Otherwise, the court will have to decide what disposition will be made of the money, now in Leaksville bank."

"Mr. Turner had known for a long time that Wagner was in Tennessee and he has had voluminous correspondence with the sheriffs' here regarding that man."

Well, from what that said, it looked to me like the officer's story that they just happened to run across Wagner kind of accidentally like and he started shooting, didn't make too much sense. But I figured I'd find out the truth of the matter by going to the trial and hearing it for myself.

I got to Blountville early, but there was already a crowd around the courthouse. Cars were parked all the way back down the road to the bridge, and more were coming all the time. I knew a feller who lived there, so I drove over to his house, which was just a block off the main road on a side street, and asked him if I could park my car out behind his barn. He charged me fifty cents, which I figured was a mite high, but I knew I'd get it back after the trial was over, because he said he had to work, and couldn't go, and I knew he wanted me to tell him all about it, and I'd get my money back then or I wouldn't tell him a blamed thing.

Still, with a crowd like there was coming in, I knew that there would be a real problem getting some place to park, and I don't like to leave my car parked right along the road, because you never know when somebody is going to smack into you and mess up your paint.

I walked back over to the courthouse and joined the crowd. The judge drove up about then, and couldn't find any place to park his car. He kept trying to get a place in back of the courthouse, but cars were already thick in there. He finally stopped in the middle of the road and hollered to somebody in the crowd to go get the sheriff for him.

Cars were lining up behind his car, and tooting their horns for him to get out of the way. Some of them sat there and raced their engines, which just added to the noise and confusion but the judge didn't budge an inch.

I don't know Judge Chase, but they tell me he is a good man, and a fair judge. He has just taken over the criminal court in Sullivan County.

But from where I stood watching him, I could see his face getting redder by the minute as he sat there in his car in the middle of the road and the crowd and waited for the sheriff to come out to him.

The tooting horns and racing engines didn't help any either. And when one loud mouth starting yelling for him to move on, I thought for a minute he was going to get out of his car and lamblast somebody for sure. A deputy sheriff came hurrying through the crowd and went out to Judge Chase's car.

The Judge got out and the deputy got in and drove the car away to park it some place. Judge Chase was carrying some books and papers and things under his arm, and he started pushing his way through the crowd toward the courthouse.

His face was still red, and he looked like he was somewhat put out by the way things had gone.

I was standing fairly close to the courthouse doors by that time, having sort of elbowed my way through the crowd, and I heard the judge tell another deputy to rope off a parking space for him as soon as one was vacant, and to make it right beside the courthouse, too.

"I intend to keep order here," he told the deputy. "Both inside the courtroom and outside, for that matter." Trying to squeeze into the courtroom was no easy task. People were crowded in the halls, outside on the porch, on the lawn and even on the street. And it was only a little past 8 o'clock in the morning.

I nosed around a little bit and listened here and there as well as I could, and found out that the judge wasn't going to convene court until 10 o'clock, nearly two hours away.

Seeing all them people crowded in and around the courthouse had got me to thinking. I never heard of a court yet that didn't recess for

45

lunch, and there was going to be a lot of mighty hungry people trying to find something to eat when that happened.

After thinking about it some, I went back outside and hunted up a telephone down at the drug store and called this feller I happened to know in Bristol.

"I need you to get up an order for me and deliver it," I told him.

"Why, sure. Be glad to. You in Kingsport?"

"No, I'm here in Blountville. I want you to make up an order of 500 hamburgers and bring them down here at noon. I think I can sell them fast."

"Five-hundred? Man, you must be out of your mind. There ain't that many people live in Blountville all together!"

"Never mind, I'll pay for them. What are you getting for a hamburger at your lunch counter?"

He dickered around some and finally admitted that he was selling hamburgers for a nickel each and making money at it. I told him I would pay him 6 cents each, delivered, but he would have to wrap them in paper napkins so they would stay warm.

"It's a deal," he chortled, gleefully. "And you'll pay cash?"

I did some quick figuring and told him yes, the money would be waiting on him as soon as he could get here. I double checked to make sure that I had $30 in cash with me, and I did, so I went over and hunted up Joe Crum, who was just loafing around his house, and hired him to meet the hamburger man and pay him, and then sell the hamburgers to the hungry crowd for 15 cents each. I promised him 10 dollars for the day's work, so he was down right enthused.

I knew there wouldn't be any problem in selling the 500 hamburgers and that more would probably be called for, but there ain't no use in being greedy. If they all sold as fast as I figured they would, I'd make an even thirty dollars out of the deal, not counting the telephone call, which cost me a nickel, and the time I used to think up the idea, which didn't cost me anything at all.

And besides, it would cost the folks more than 15 cents per hamburger to get one if they had to drive all the way to Bristol, which they would if they didn't want to buy mine.

Having gotten that little bit of business taken care of, I worked my way back through the crowd and inside the courthouse.

The halls were full, and every office seemed packed with people. I managed to inch my way along toward the courtroom and, by degrees, got inside. Every seat was taken, and both men and women were already standing along the sides and in the back.

People tend to move toward the back of the room when they go in, sort of like they are embarrassed to take the first row of seats or stand near the front. It is as if though they felt very conspicuous there, sensing every eye behind them turned on the back of their necks. It didn't bother me. I learned long ago that the least noticeable place is right up front, because everybody behind you is looking beyond you at the judge, or witness, or whoever might be performing at the time.

The last place in the world that people look for a seat or standing room is up front. I walked up there, and, sure enough, there was one empty seat, beside this fat lady.

When I went over and sat down in it, she glared up at me.

"Young man," she said, "I am saving this seat for my sister," she said. "She will be here soon."

"Well, I think that's nice," I told her. "You got a receipt for it?"

"What do you mean, receipt?"

"Well, what I mean is that since it is public property and you are saving it, you must own it. And if you own it, you must have bought it. And if you bought it, you ought to have a receipt."

"Well, I never!" she exclaimed

"I didn't figure you did," I said. That sort of ended the conversation.

I made up my mind that if the sister showed up and was a frail old lady or a nice looking one, I would be a gentleman and let her have the seat and go stand by the wall. But after judging the blood lines and bone structure of the fat woman beside me, I didn't worry too much over it.

If her sister was built on the same pattern, standing up would be the best thing for her, because it might help her lose a pound or two.

It took a long time for things to get started on the trial. Lawyers kept coming in and going out, and the judge stuck his head in through the door from his private office a time or two, I guess to see if they were all ready. When he saw that the lawyers were still shuffling papers and things and talking to each other, he would close the door back and wait another little while before he peeked out again.

At long last, about 10 o'clock, he opened the door and came out. The bailiff jumped up and hollered out that "oyez, oyez, oyez" business they always do when the judge takes the bench, and declared that the court was now in session, the Right Honorable Judge Guy S. Chase presiding.

Kinnie Wagner and his two lawyers, Burrows and Warren, entered the bullpen of the courtroom from the other door, toward the jail cells, and took seats at the defense table up front.

Attorney General Lovette came in with Worley and Luke McAmis and sat at the other table. A few minutes later, T. R. Bandy came hurrying in and joined them.

There were two or three other chairs around the prosecutor's table, waiting for other volunteer lawyers from Kingsport to fill them. From the talk I picked up on the streets, dang near every lawyer in Kingsport who didn't have anything else to do at the moment had decided to help prosecute Wagner, figuring that it would be good publicity because they might get their names in the paper, or get seen by a whole bunch of people at one time, inside the crowded courtroom.

Lawyers make their money by getting clients, and the best way to get clients is to be known by a lot of people, and the only way you can get a lot of people to know you is to be seen by a lot of people, so I reckoned they figured right about that.

Judge Chase made kind of a little speech about what the trial was going to be about and all, and how important it was that people do their duty as citizens and serve on the jury, because everybody who was accused of a crime was entitled to a trial by jury, whether they had done the crime or not, which sounded like a sort of waste of time to me, but not being a lawyer and all, I wouldn't know.

I looked at Wagner closely, because he was sitting just a few feet from me. He didn't look nearly as mean as I expected. In fact, he looked just like an everyday sort of chap, and even seemed friendly enough.

He smiled and nodded now and then while talking to his lawyers, and he didn't seem nervous nor angry, nor anything like that at all.

Now and then, he would look out over the crowd in the courtroom and smile and kind of nod his head at somebody he knew. I saw his lips move in a "hello' a time or two.

Well, first crack out of the box, when the judge said that court was convened, Lawyer Warren jumps up and makes a motion that the case be continued to a later term of court, and all the lawyers at the prosecution table jumped up, knocking over one chair and nearly two others, and started hollering out objections, and Judge Chase banged his gavel down on the bench and called for order.

Wagner's other lawyer, Burrows, got up, too, and they went at it hot and heavy for a spell.

The fat lady's sister never did show up. Or if she did, she never did get all the way up to the front of the courtroom where we were sitting, so I didn't have to worry about giving up my seat to her, whatever her condition might have been.

The lawyers for the defense and the lawyers for the prosecution went at it hot and heavy for the longest time. Burrows and Warren kept claiming that they had not had enough time to adequately prepare the case, and Lovette and the rest of them kept arguing that it didn't make no difference, because Wagner admitted that he had done the killing, and that all the facts were known, and the trial should go on as scheduled. All of them got to put their two cents worth in, I believe.

I noticed that the Kingsport lawyers, when they got up to say something talked toward the judge but looked toward the crowd, as much as they could, which sort of confirmed what I had already figured out about how participating in the trial was mighty good advertising for their business.

Wagner was on trial in this case for the murder of John F. Smith, one of the policemen who had been killed. The other dead officer, Webb, wasn't being mentioned much, because they would have another trial about that after this one was finished, the judge said.

One top of that, there was to be a third trial, for assault with a deadly weapon with intent to kill, on account of the officer who was wounded and the one who got shot at, if he really did.

And, if they didn't convict him of none of those, I overheard some of the deputies talking about how they was going to send him back down to Mississippi to stand trial for murder there, where they claimed he had shot and killed a deputy sheriff named MacIntosh.

It didn't seem to be worrying Wagner. He was taking it all in, sort of like he was enjoying the proceedings. He was wearing a blue serge suit, which looked new, and a white shirt and collar with a blue tie, like he was dressed to go to a party or at least to a high falutin' church meeting of some sort. Clean shaven, Wagner's hair was carefully combed and very neat, wavy and dark, and he looked a whole lot better than most of the lawyers and all the deputies who were milling around.

And he didn't seem a blamed bit upset. I heard that you can tell how nervous a person is by the number of times they blink their eyes in a minute. I watched as closely as I could, and couldn't catch him blinking at all. Maybe I was too far away, or perhaps it was the way he had of kind of squeezing his eyes narrow now and then, but I sure didn't see none.

He kept leaning over for whispered conversations with his lawyers, first to the one on the left and then with the one on the right, but he watched everything intently and paid very close attention to every word being spoken.

I thought they'd never get through arguing over it. But finally, just as everybody in the courtroom was beginning to squirm around some in their seats, except for the lawyers and Wagner, on account of it was getting nigh onto noon and the hungry pangs were beginning to hit, the judge ups and says that he is going to overrule the motion for a continuance and adjourn for lunch.

Burrows and Warren jumped up and said "Exception!" almost in one voice, and Judge Chase looked at them for a minute and said that their exception was noted.

Then he said that the court would recess for lunch until one o'clock, at which time the jury selection would begin, and sort of warned that everybody that had been called as veniremen had best be on hand at that time in case they got called.

People started pouring out of the courtroom doors before Judge Chase could even bang his gavel down to make it official.

People always seem to jump up and try to get out the door at the same time, then they have to stand there and wait in line, with their feet hurting, until the crowd thins out and they can inch through.

It's like that at the movies, and at church and revivals and political meetings, and just about every place where there is a crowd of people who get turned loose at the same time. All of them seem to have the same idea, that they have to get out of whatever place they are in, and that they have got to do it right away, so they bunch up and get in each other's way, and get their corns stepped on, and get pushed and shoved and crowded something awful.

If the building was on fire, you could sort of expect it, I guess, but the way lots of folks go about getting out would get a bunch of them burned up for sure if it was.

The fat lady beside me was no exception. She jumped up even before the judge could get out of his chair and bounced along toward the door. Of course, a couple of dozen people got there first, and she had to wait, which must have been a burden to her poor feet, seeing as

50

she had to weigh more than they were equipped to carry, but that's what she done.

Everybody else in there did the same thing, except me. I knew there wasn't a bit of use in trying to get out the door ahead of the crowd, so I just sat and waited until the courtroom kind of cleared out, and it was a whole lot easier.

The hall was still crowded, but not so much that you couldn't squeeze through.

People were standing around, trying to make up their minds about what they should do about dinner. Most of them hadn't thought that far ahead. They had come to the trial out of curiosity and excitement, and hadn't taken time to realize that their stomachs didn't share the same interests, and would get ideas of their own about mealtime.

Outside, I saw a bunch of people crowded around a truck parked in the middle of the road, and I knew right then that my load of hamburgers from Bristol had arrived....

It liked to have caused a riot!

People were crowding around the truck where the hamburgers were, buying them as fast as Joe Crum could take their money or make change.

A few people got mad over the price and turned away, saying they'd be blamed if they was going to pay no fifteen cents for a hamburger sandwich, which probably didn't have enough mustard on it anyways, and they would stomp off down the street, trying to find something else for dinner.

The grocery store down the road a piece did a great business in canned sardines and crackers that day, I heard later, and what cold bottled pop they had went quickly.

One or two people tried buying cans of beans or peaches and getting the storekeeper to open them up for them, but they had to buy spoons or use their pocket knives to eat them with and it didn't work out so well. The truck was stopped right in the middle of the road and so many people were crowded around it to get hamburgers that no other cars could get past.

And the judge got in his car, which the deputy had moved for him and had parked up on the lawn beside the courthouse itself, but with a sign saying "Official Court Cars Only," to keep other people from parking there too... and he couldn't get it pulled back out into the road for all the people in the way out in the middle of the street buying my hamburgers.

51

I was standing in the crowd where I could see him, and I never seen a man's face get so red before in my life!

It was a nice day, but he had the windows of his car fastened up tight, with them little snaps that close the side curtains so well, and he got to pushing on the side curtain to open it up so he could yell at folks to get out of the way, and he must have pushed too hard, because his whole hand butted right through the side curtain and stuck out, like it was kind of surprised, in the air beside his car.

He jerked at the car door to open it and the handle come off in his hand, and I thought for a minute there that it was a good thing that he was not behind the bench right now with a prisoner before him who had made him that mad, because he would probably sentence the man to a million years of being hung, he was so put out.

The crowd was kind of carrying me along toward the judge's car, and when I got close enough to hear him talk, he was yelling for a deputy to come and disperse the crowd and to arrest whoever it was that had caused it, and to do it right now!

It all blew over, though.

I managed to get through the crowd to the truck where Joe Crum was selling the hamburgers just as a feller pulled his car out of a parking space down the road a few feet, and I got in the cab and moved the vehicle into that spot while Joe kept handing out the hamburgers and taking money and making change.

The judge got his car pulled out and drove off, with his face as red as a ripe tomato.

He knocked over the sign the deputy had put up that said "Official Court Cars Only," and drove right over it, never even looking back.

The crowd was thinning out some now, but parking spaces along the road were still mighty scarce. I looked up as a car drove past, going slow, like he was looking for a parking spot, and it was that blamed smart alec in his yellow Buick again.

He spotted the place where Judge Chase had been parked, because you could still see the tire marks on the grass. He got out, kind of strutting around, and walked inside the courthouse, probably to get a good seat in the courtroom while everybody else was out eating and the place was empty.

I didn't pay any more attention because I was busy helping Joe with selling the hamburgers. They were all gone in about 30 minutes, except for one I remembered to stick in my pocket to eat myself, because I just remembered that I would have to have some lunch myself, and I never did like them blamed sardines and cracker lunches you have to get at a country store.

We counted up our money, and I paid off Joe, like I'd promised, and paid myself back the original $30 I'd given him to pay the man from Bristol, and I found out that I had made $27 out of the whole deal, which was $3 short of what I should have made, but pretty good after all.

I never did figure out what happened to that other three dollars. It could have been lost in making change, or a few of the people crowded around could have grabbed up hamburgers without paying for them, or the fellow from Bristol could have shorted me by a few. It didn't matter much, and I sure wasn't going to lose any sleep over it. Any time I can make $27 out of a possible fifty bucks' profit, I'll suffer the $3 loss willingly.

Joe Crum was all excited about having made ten dollars so fast and easy. He wanted to know if I was going to do the same thing the next day, and I told him we would, but for him to get up early the next morning and drive his old truck over and park it along the road close to the courthouse before anybody else got there, and then just leave it, so we wouldn't block the road again and make the judge even madder than he already was. I dug the hamburger out of my pocket and ate it. It tasted kind of like old sawdust, but was better than nothing.

I checked my watch and saw that it was nearly one o'clock, and that court would be convening as soon as the judge got back, so I started back to the courthouse.

I was almost at the door when I heard this car horn start to blast.

It was the usual "ougooogha" type of horn and whoever was setting it off was sure sticking with it.

I looked back out toward the road, and there was the judge, in his car, out in the roadway, trying to get into his reserved parking space, where that blamed yellow Buick was setting, like a big lump on a log!

The judge's face was red again. It looked like you could start a fire by touching a piece of paper to it.

A deputy came running over through the crowd, and the judge jumped out of his car and starting hollering for him to get that car moved, and to impound it, and to haul it around the back of the jail and lock it up, even if he had to chain the wheels to a tree or something, and to arrest the owner for contempt of court when he even showed up to claim it.

He stomped off through the crowd, heading toward the courthouse, and I ducked inside ahead of him, working my way through the now sparce crowd to the courtroom, where I went back to the same seat I had sat in that morning. People usually go back to the same seats, I've noticed. It is as if they have laid claim to the territory and plan to set up housekeeping there. But that feeling only lasts for the one day, and, if they have to visit the same place again the following day, they will take other seats, better ones if they can get them, without even thinking about it.

The judge must have gone into his private chambers through another door or hallway.

The crowd starting drifting back, and before long, the seats were all filled and the walls crowded, just like before.

The fat lady had reclaimed the seat beside mine, but she didn't even mention her sister this time, and I didn't either.

The lawyers came back in and took seats at the table. Then the judge came out, and right after him, through another door, two deputies came in with Wagner. They all got settled and seated, and the bailiff got a nod from Judge Chase and called court to order again, and they jumped right into selecting a jury from the 100-man venire that had been called.

The first man called up admitted that he had already formed an opinion and felt that Wagner was guilty. So they turned him down, which I didn't think he minded much, and called another man.

It was on the third try that they got a juryman both sides would accept. His name was W. M. Jones, and he said he was a farmer, and from the 20th Civil District.

He hadn't read anything about the case, hadn't heard anything much about it, except for what had been said to him today in Blountville, and didn't know either Wagner or any of the officers who had been shot or killed.

I figured if they was going to have to find folks like Jones, who didn't know a blamed thing about the shootings, they were in for a long day, and I was right about that.

It dragged on for ever so long.

They'd call a prospective juryman, and both sides would question him. The folks who seemed in favor of the prosecution got challenged by the defense and the folks who seemed in favor of the defendant were objected to by the prosecution.

About four out of five called were turned down for some reason or another.

By three o'clock that afternoon, they had managed to select just four jurymen out of about 20 or so they had questioned.

I made notes in a little note pad I had with me, and the men selected for jury duty at that time were the farmer, Jones; E. L. King, also a farmer, and of the 20th Civil District; W. R. Anderson, of Bristol, Tennessee, who worked as a clerk at the W. E. King Company there in Bristol; and E. M. Kaylor, who said he was a retail grocerman of Bristol, Tennessee.

Sheriff W. J. Turner of Greene County, Mississippi, was in the courtroom as a spectator. He sat just about two people down from me, in the middle of the front row bench on the left side of the courtroom.

My guess was that he had come to the trial in case they decided some way to turn Wagner back over to him, and let him be taken back to Mississippi to stand trial for killing the MacIntosh feller there.

You could tell that Sheriff Turner felt real important, and that he thought all eyes were on him, but I didn't see nobody paying too much attention to him myself.

During one recess of the court a couple of officers come up and talked to Turner some.

They were apparently asking about that $1,000 reward and about who was to get it, and how it would be paid and all, and Sheriff Turner told them he just didn't know.

He said the reward money had been donated in nickels and dimes and dollars from people all over Greene County, Mississippi, and that it had been stipulated that it was to be paid for the capture of Kinnie Wagner, dead or alive, to stand trial in Mississippi.

It looked to me like offering a reward for somebody dead or alive would be about the same as hiring somebody killed, and that the people who put up the money would be doing something illegal, but I'm no lawyer, and I guess I don't understand these things.

Wagner looked back at Sheriff Turner and smiled a time or two. I could see the sheriff's face get red ever time he done it. That man was mad at Wagner, there was no question about that, and if Wagner ever got turned over to his custody, I wouldn't give you two cents for his chances of ever getting inside a courtroom for another trial.

Turner told the officers that if Wagner was convicted and executed for the murders he was charged with, it was possible that his body

55

could then be turned over to Mississippi, through himself, and the $1,000 might be collected.

But he never did say for sure.

By 3 o'clock that afternoon, I was plumb tuckered out. There is something about setting in a courtroom, listening to a trial and all the arguing that goes on by the lawyers and the judge that just wears you down. I figured I wouldn't miss anything, because from the way they were going at it, the jury wouldn't all get picked before 5 or 6 o'clock, and the judge would probably recess for the day shortly after that.

So I slipped out of the courtroom and walked back over to where I'd left my car.

On the way out of the courthouse, I did see that yellow Buick had been removed, somehow, and the judge's car was parked back in its place, with the "Court Officials' Cars Only" sign back up.

I glanced around the corner of the courthouse toward the jail cells, which are at the back, but I didn't see any sign of the Buick. Of course, it could have been pulled inside, because I understand they've got a garage door back there the sheriff sometimes uses.

That smart alec was going to have some tall explaining to do to Judge Guy Chase, I reckoned. Even if he didn't see the judge's sign and parked in that spot through ignorance, the judge didn't appear to be a man who was too prone to forgiveness.

I picked up my car over at Johnson's house and headed back toward Kingsport.

They have started working on the road in Blountville, and a good-sized stretch of it has been graded and widened through the middle of town. Cars were parked lining both sides, all the way out of sight. I judged that the line of parked cars stretched a good half-mile back toward Kingsport, and my guess was that it would have been even longer in the other direction.

Just a few years ago, I had driven Jay Fred Johnson and George Eastman over this same road, but it was a lot more narrow and crooked in those days. Chestnut Hill is still a tough one to pull, however, and widening it out didn't seem to be a whole lot of help. You often see cars parked along side of that steep, winding road, steam pouring out of overheated radiators, while the frantic driver fans at the heat with his hand or hat, as if that would do any good.

This time however, I had the road just about to myself.

Old man Huggins was poking along about halfway up in a wagon pulled by a team of mules, but there was room to get by and I passed him without any trouble at all.

When I got to the top of Chestnut Ridge, I kicked her out of gear and coasted down toward Dead Man's Curve.

You can really save gas that way, but a lot of folks are afraid to try it, because they get scared their engine won't start up again when they need it on account of getting so cooled off by the wind and all, that is a bunch of nonsense, for I have never got stalled and I've done it plenty of times.

The car, without the engine running, was a kind of silent sailboat, skimming across the ground and down the hill like a big coaster wagon, the whistling wind the only sound. It felt almost like that blamed airplane ride I took one time, except it wasn't as noisy, and not so far up either.

I was really enjoying the ride down the hill until that blamed "thing" was right smack-dab out in the middle of the road up ahead.

At first glance, I thought it was a drag sled. But I saw right away that the slope on what I had first taken for runners was too steep.

It was a big, box-like thing, about 6 feet high and 10 feet long, made of gray, weathered boards. The sloped end went up at a fairly sharp pitch, making the top side about a foot or so longer than the bottom.

It had a log chain tied around its middle, and the chain was hitched to a mule, who was slowly dragging it across the roadway.

A dad-blamed privy! I slammed on the foot brake as hard as I could, standing up on it to get more pressure, and pulled the hand brake at the same time.

My car, with the engine not running due to my coasting down the hill, went into a skid in the loose gravel on the road, and I shot toward the horizontal outhouse like a baseball hit by Babe Ruth.

There was no way to avoid hitting the blamed thing, and that is just what I did, smacking right into the side of it with the crash and creak and groan of breaking boards.

A couple of the side-boards busted and kind of stuck up on the radiator of my car, and I never heard such yelling in my life as there was coming from inside of it.

The momentum of the car knocked the thing eight or ten feet down the road, with the car skidding right along with it to come to a dusty stop just as the door, which was horizontal on the top side, flew up and old man Jarvis stuck his head out.

"What the devil is going on?" he yelled.

Clem Jarvis, his oldest son, came running up, the mule's reins still in his hand. "Are ya hurt, Pa?" he hollered.

"I dunno," the old man yelled back. "I don't reckon. Whut the tarnation happened anyway?"

I got out of the car and got it all sorted out finally. What had happened was that the Jarvises had built a new house across the road from their old one, after the old roof got to leaking so bad they couldn't get it fixed. But they had not yet built a new privy on the new side of the road, because the old man was in the habit of spending a lot of time in the old one, which had a view down the hill toward Kingsport that he liked to look at, and so they just walked across the road and up on the hill when the need arose.

But the past winter's snow had been more than Ma Jarvis was willing to put up with, and she demanded that the privy be moved across the road to the new house, view or not, or a new one be constructed, before she would make any more hot biscuits for breakfast. So Clem had hitched the chain to the structure and pulled it over, dragging it across the road to the new location on the edge of a gully.

None of them realized that Pa Jarvis was inside the blamed thing and had nodded off to nap time while reading the Sears and Roebuck Catalog that was there for other purposes.

We got it all straightened out in a little while. Nobody was hurt, and the privy wasn't damaged too much. Jarvis said he figured he could just nail a couple of boards on the busted side of it and hardly anybody would ever notice that it had been in a wreck.

My car wasn't banged up to amount to anything, although the front bumper got the mud knocked off of it. So I headed on downtown and for home, because I sure wanted to get an early start the next morning.

I put my car into the garage and locked it up. As I walked home, I remembered that it was Tuesday night, and that meant beef stew and hot biscuits at the boarding house table, so I forgot all about the trial and other stuff and quickened my pace. If there's anything I hate to do, it is show up late for a boarding house meal. The other boarders are crowded around the table, busy eating, and they don't like to take time to pass things, so you have to grab for yourself.

It may have taken nearly five thousand years to get man civilized, like some of the preachers say, but being late for a boarding house meal will uncivilize them in a matter of minutes.

So I was glad that I got there before they started putting the food on the table.

My prediction had been right. I could smell the beef stew as soon as I walked down the hall. Of course, the kitchen door was open and that helped, but there was no mistaking that delicious aroma. My landlady uses a lot of onions and garlic, with, she told me at one time, just a few drops of tarragon vinegar, which really puts the flavor to it. And hot biscuits...my! That woman knows how to bake.

I sat in the parlor with the other boarders for a few minutes before we were called to the table, and we talked about events of the day. One of the fellows had been to the trial as well, and he told all about it. He hadn't seen me, because I was setting right up front, and hardly anybody ever notices you there, so I just kept still and let him tell about it.

Then the landlady called "Dinner" and we all made a rush for the table, and got down to the serious business of shoveling in food.

I was up early the following morning and got to Blountville before the crowd started coming in.

There were already a few cars parked here and there on the main road, and I saw that Joe Crum had left the truck parked there as near the front of the courthouse as he could get it, so there would be better lunch time sales of hamburgers, because folks could get to it from the sidewalk area instead of having to get out in the road again. I say sidewalk area, because that is where they will probably put sidewalks someday when they have them. Right now, there is a gravel path on each side of the road, which is just as good, except not as smooth and it gets mighty wet in the rainy season.

I decided to cut down a little on my hamburger order, because a lot of folks might bring a sandwich or something with them today, instead of buying whatever they could get like they had to do that first day. So I called my friend in Bristol and cut the order down to 250. That would still be enough to bring in $37.50, at a cost of $12.50 to me, plus the $10 a day I was paying Joe to sell them, and should leave me with $12.50 clear, which was enough to make up for hauling business I might be losing by setting around at the Wagner trial like I was doing.

As it turned out, I was mighty glad I had done that, but that come up later, when the court recessed for lunch. I went inside the

59

courthouse and walked around the halls, waiting for people to start showing up. It wasn't long before folks started coming in, and I noticed a lot of them carrying dinner buckets this time. That's one thing about Sullivan County folks, you can catch them unaware one time and they will allow you to do it. But the next time, if they fall for the same stunt, they figure it is their own fault, and they don't like for that to happen.

Thinking about that, I sort of was sorry that I hadn't just canceled the whole hamburger order and let Joe go, but I'd made enough profit to risk one more venture before I got out of the food business, so I decided to play a pat hand one more time.

The place filled up by 9 o'clock. I had gone inside and taken the same seat as the day before, and just a few minutes after I sat down, the other folks started pouring in.

Judge Chase arrived and the door that leads back to the jail cells opened and Wagner came in with his two lawyers and a deputy sheriff.

The prosecution lawyers came down through the courtroom and took their seats at the other table, and Judge Chase called court to order, and they got right into it.

It seems that they had finally got all the jurors picked after I left the day before, and they came in and took their seats in the jury box.

Before they could get going on the trial, one of the jurors jumped up and asks if he can talk to the judge, and Chase told him to go ahead.

"Yer Honor," he drawled, looking worried and scared at the same time, "I think I need to talk to you." "Yes sir," the judge said. "What is the problem?"

"Well, I didn't understand what these lawyers meant when they asked me if I wuz again capital punishment," the man said. "And now, somebody told me that capital punishment means putting a man in the 'lectric chair and killing him if he is convicted. I can't do that. That's killing and the Good Book is again it."

"Now let me understand," Judge Chase said. "You find that you have moral convictions against capital punishment, is that right?"

"Well, do capital punishment mean killing him?"

"Yes."

"Then yes, I'm again it. I shore wouldn't want to have to do that."

"Very well," the Judge said. "You are excused. Do we have an alternate already qualified?"

For once they did. They not only had an alternate juror already qualified, but an alternate's alternate, so the man opposed to capital punishment came out of the jury box and another juror was seated in his place. "Mr. Lovette," Judge Chase said, "call your first witness."

The attorney general cleared his throat and got to his feet.

"The state calls," he announced in a clear, ringing voice, "Deputy Sheriff Joe Groseclose..."

Deputy Groseclose testified that after he had seen Policeman Smith fall to the ground, and had hit the dirt himself after hearing more shots coming at him, and had seen a red sweater through the trees and bushes, he lay there for a minute, then he summoned help.

He testified that he and another man took the pistols from the dead men. He swore that neither of Smith's pistols had been fired, and that Webb's had been fired only once.

In the examination of Smith's body, he said, Groseclose found the pistols both still in their holsters, and, he said, both of the holsters were under Smith's uniform coat, which was buttoned up.

That caused a stir in the courtroom and the Judge called for order.

Wagner kept looking right at Groseclose's face and smiling that cool smile of his, and the deputy's eyes would dart away each time they happened to glance at the desperado.

The lawyers all got up and argued about the witness' testimony. The defense was objecting that there was no proper ground work for the witness' claim that the coat was buttoned up or something like that, and the prosecution lawyers argued that there was. Judge Chase ruled for the prosecution, and they got on with it.

The Bristol lawyers who were defending Wagner cross-examined Groseclose, but couldn't get him to make any big changes in his story, and finally told him to come down.

After Groseclose, they called Deputy George Miller. He said that he and the other officers had gone to the river that afternoon because of a telephone call to the effect that there was some disorder down there. Before going to the river, he said, the officers had divided their forces, with Frazier and himself going straight across the field to the river while the others went on further down the road and across.

While he and Frazier were walking down the river path, Miller said, he glanced downstream and saw someone. "I saw a man rise up," he said. "He had on a sweater and a bright cap and I saw him raise something in his hand and I said to Frazier .. Look out!"

Then, the man shot, and Frazier fell, Miller said.

Deputy Miller testified that no other shots had been fired prior to the one that brought Frazier down. He said that Frazier grabbed himself and said "I'm shot!"

Miller swore that Frazier never fired his gun, but that he, himself, pulled out his pistol and fired a shot at the man who shot Frazier. He also said that up until the time Frazier was shot, no other shots had been fired down the river.

Defense Attorney George M. Warren then put Miller through a grueling cross-examination.

"Isn't it true," Warren roared at him, "that you officers went down there deliberately to capture or kill Kinnie Wagner?"

"No." Miller said.

"You had heard that he was down there, hadn't you?" Warren went on.

"No, I hadn't heard that. Not for sure."

"What do you mean, not for sure?" Warren demanded.

"Well, I might have heard some talk about Wagner being around town, but that was all," Miller said. "I didn't even know that he was in this part of the country, not for sure."

"But you had heard that he was?"

"Well, I might have heard it, but I didn't know it. There's a big difference," Miller said.

Warren bore down on him pretty hard. But Miller denied about everything that Warren accused him of. He insisted that no other shots had been fired, and that he didn't know that Wagner was there, or anywhere around at all, and that when the first shot was fired, he didn't turn and run back up the river, like Warren kept asking him if he did.

But the entire courtroom kind of jarred to a tense silence when Warren stopped and looked out toward the crowd, his back to Miller. He stood there silently for a few seconds, which seemed like much longer, and suddenly wheeled around and pointed a finger at Miller.

"Isn't it true," he roared, "that you stopped a man on the Bluff City Highway and made him put up a cash bond, and then failed to turn in the cash?"

Oh, man, did that kick over the beehive.

All the prosecution attorneys ... Lovette, Bandy, McAmis and the others jumped to their feet, knocking over chairs and shouting objections.

Judge Chase had to bang his gavel down hard several times to get things quieted down.

I sort of figured out what Warren was trying to do. If he could get the jury to thinking the officers were what you'd call "fee grabbers," which most officers these days are said to be, and if the jury believed that they often cheated on the county by keeping cash bonds and other fees for themselves, like folks say a lot of them do, he might be able to cast a good bit of doubt on the accuracy of their testimony.

After all, if a man lies about money, isn't it likely that he will lie about other things as well?

Judge Chase finally said he was going to uphold the objection, because the question was not pertinent to the testimony or something like that, and it was approaching the noon hour and he was going to recess for lunch, and that court would reconvene at one in the afternoon, sharp, and he banged down his gavel and got up and walked out of the courtroom through his private door.

The crowd all jumped up at once and started for the doorways. The halls were still kind of crowded, even though most people had already gone outside by the time I got out of the courtroom.

Outside, I looked over beside the road, and saw Joe Crum was selling hamburgers. He still had a pile of them, all nicely wrapped up, on a big tray he had put up in the bed of the truck, but there were still enough people around to where it didn't look like I'd get stuck with too many unsold hamburgers.

Folks were seated on benches here and there, eating their lunches. Many of them had brought dinner buckets, and were eating chicken legs and even hunks of cornbread and such. I decided right then and there not to do it again the next day.

After the crowd died down a little, I went over to the truck and me and Joe counted up the leavings. We still had a couple of dozen hamburgers left, but Joe had taken in $33.90, which was right up to snuff the way I counted. I paid him the $10 I had promised, plus the $12.50 I paid the fellow from Bristol who made them and brought them down, and I had cleared $13.80, besides the 2 dozen hamburgers that were left. I ate one myself, then took the others to the jailhouse and told the jailer to give them to the fellows who were locked up. I figured they might kind of like a change from the regular cornbread-and-bean diet Sullivan County has grown famous for.

That's where I saw the yellow Buick again. It was locked up in a shed behind the jail.

The reason I noticed it was that I was walking past the shed, after having given the extra hamburgers to the jailer, and my shoe came untied. I knelt down to tie it, and just happened to glance toward the crack between the hinges and the wall.

Judge Chase must have made good on that threat to confiscate the car when it was in his private parking space! I peeked through the crack, and there it was, alright. So I walked back over to the jail and asked the deputy about it.

"That car?" he said. "The judge ordered it locked up. He said he is going to have it sold if the owner doesn't come and claim it, and we are to arrest the owner for contempt of court if he does show up."

I hadn't seen the smart-alec who had been driving it the last day or two, but it was pretty obvious that he had been afraid to come and get his car, so he must have known all about it.

"When is it to be sold?" I asked.

"The judge didn't say. I'd guess he will hold it for 90 days or something like that, and then order it sold. The owner may come and get it, of course."

I filed that bit of information in my head and walked back to the courthouse. When the trial started up again that afternoon, the main witnesses were Sheriff Joe Thomas and a local policeman, W. W. Leedy.

Thomas testified that on the morning after the tragedy, he asked Wagner how he came to do such a terrible thing, and the prisoner replied that he saw them coming and thought they were after him, and he got them first.

The examination and cross-examination of Thomas was very brief. Neither the prosecution nor the defense seemed very much inclined to try and draw it out.

Officer Leedy took the stand then, and said he talked to Wagner in an automobile while going to Blountville on the morning of the desperado's arrest. Leedy said he asked Wagner which officer shot first and Wagner told him he saw two men coming down the river toward him, one in uniform, and that he shot the one in uniform.

Leedy said that Wagner told him that he then heard someone down the river and that he turned and shot at another man in uniform in that direction.

"He said he shot first," Officer Leedy declared.

Leedy testified that Wagner further stated to him that he shot the man on the bank, but didn't know whether or not he killed him.

That wrapped up the court session for the day, and the judge adjourned early, saying that court would reconvene at 9 o'clock sharp the following morning.

I headed back to Kingsport as soon as I got through the crowd and to my car.

It was a nice spring day, with warm sunshine and no wind to speak of, and I enjoyed the drive back home. I had not much more than pulled up to a stop on Market Street, planning to go to Nick's Restaurant for supper, when Roy Pyle came by. He was heading to his car, which was parked just a little further down the street. When he saw me, he came over.

"Hello Pug," he said. "I just came out of the newspaper office. I've been telling them about what happened over in Scott County."

Roy was excited, I could tell by the way he was talking.

"It was terrible," he said, "from what they said. I got the story from T. H. Nickels, but everybody over there was talking about it. "They found this woman with her head off. It was at a house 7 miles from Gate City. Name of Ervin. Mrs. Joe Ervin. Her head had been completely severed."

"Over on Copper Creek, it was. They looked around the house some, and then they found Joe Ervin in the smokehouse.

He had evidently hanged hisself. They didn't find him until about two hours after they found his wife. They figure that Ervin must have killed her by cutting her head off like that, and then went out to the smokehouse and committed suicide by hanging hisself. They don't know for sure just when it happened, but they think they had been dead for several days, so it must have happened a week or so back."

Roy went on to say that he had gone over to Gate City on business, and that everybody over there was talking about it, so he had got as many details as he could and then come back and went to the newspaper office and told them about it so they could print it.

He went on to his car, just sort of shaking his head over such things happening in our area, and I sat there for awhile and thought about the same thing myself.

Grim Verdict

I saw Jay Fred that evening. He had left word at Nick's that he wanted me to stop by because he had something he wanted to talk to me about.

Jay Fred's office is in what he calls "The Improvement Building," on account, I suppose, of he built it with what he called improvement company money - Kingsport Improvement Company money, that is. What happened was, back a few years, when Jay Fred's in-law, George L. Carter, got the idea of building the Clinchfield Railroad from Spartanburg to Chicago so he could haul his coal out of the Virginia mountains cheaper, he got a gang of rich men together and formed that outfit. They put up the cash and George L. spent it. He brought Jay Fred in to kind of run things here for him after they bought all the land and decided to build a town.

Jay Fred is a kind of local wheelhoss. He gets industrial firms to come in and build plants, lots of times on land he gives them, so there will be jobs, so storekeepers will want stores, so he can sell them lots to build the stores on. So far, it has worked out well, with the town growing and with the industrial plants getting cheaper labor than they could get up north, and with the storekeepers selling enough of their wares and goods to pay for the lots they buy, whether they make any other money or not, so Jay Fred has done all right.

He was in his office, seated behind a desk.

"Come in, Pug," he said when he saw me at the door.

"I'm glad you stopped by. I've been wanting to talk to you."

Well, when Jay Fred wants to talk to you, you can bet there is money somewhere in it. The trick is to try and get some of it instead of having to pay it. You have to be careful about that when you are dealing with a smart promoter.

What he wanted to talk about, believe it or not, was his idea of building another hospital in Kingsport. "The Riverside Hospital just isn't big enough," he said.

"Why, when that Wagner shooting thing took place, even though it was right close by, there wasn't enough room to accommodate the people who came down there to see about the officers who had been wounded or killed. They had to stand outside, and the doctor had to go out there and tell them about it." The long and short of it was that Jay Fred had found a piece of property that he thought would be a good location for a hospital, and he was trying now to figure out how to get the money to start building it.

And there were a couple of things he wanted to ask me.

Part of what Jay Fred wanted to ask me about was what was the name of the family who had lived over at Pleasant Hill, next to Gate City, that George Eastman had wanted me to drive him over to see their old home place that time a few years back when he was there making the deal to buy the old alcohol plant that later became Tennessee Eastman.

Jay Fred said he remembered me telling him about it, after I got back from taking Eastman to Bristol to catch his train, but he had been racking his brain for two days and couldn't remember the name.

Jay Fred is like that. He never really forgets anything, he just sometimes kind of misplaces it for a while, but if he can think of who to ask that does know, it brings it right back, and that is what he wanted this time.

I've watched him work and make deals like he does, and I believe that his memory is one of the things that makes it possible for him to be a wheeler-dealer like he is.

I don't know just why he wanted that name, but I guessed that it must have to do some way with his big idea about a new hospital.

"You mean the Woods family?" I asked him. "The family that had the five Confederates?"

"Woods!" he exclaimed, "Yes, that's it! Now, one of them had moved to New York, and Eastman knew him."

"Oh, yeah. He got in the real estate business up there. I guess he still is, as far as I know."

"Pug, can you remember the name of the real estate firm he was with?"

"Gee whiz, Jay Fred, that's been a long time ago, I told him, "and I don't know that I paid much attention. Eastman mentioned it, I think, when he was telling me about this feller he knew who lived here in his youth, but ... wait a minute ... I think I heard that he died. It was James Woods -James H.-that was his name. He was a railroad lawyer."

"That's the man!" Jay Fred nodded enthusiastically. "Can you remember the company name?"

"New York something - Suburban Real Estate or something like that. I just heard it mentioned that one time, but I read about the old man dying a few years ago. And if I remember right, his son had taken over the company."

Jay Fred got out a big, thick telephone directory from New York City and started reading off real estate company names. I told him I didn't have time to fool with that kind of stuff, but he insisted that I stay and help him out.

We were long down the list when he read out one that sounded familiar.

"New York Urban Real Estate," he said.

"Wait a minute," I said. "I think that's it. Yeah. I'm purty sure that was the name."

Jay Fred jumped up and got another big book off the shelf along the wall and turned a bunch of pages. "Here it is!" he almost yelled." "You're right! New York Urban Real Estate, James H. Woods..." he mumbled some more over the finer print, and looked up with a big grin.

"Pug, this may be a big help. I will call this man and talk to him. I think he may be able to help me a lot."

You never know just what Jay Fred is getting at. He works in the durndest way I've ever seen. What he does is he keeps asking folks he knows until he finds out what he wants to know, or if that won't work, until he finds out who knows what he wants to know, and then he figures out how to make them a proposition that makes them think they are getting something they want, or at least might want, that can do what they want done, and then he springs the offer on them in such a way as makes it look kind of like they thought of it, not him, and before you know it, he had got another deal all worked out to get something he wanted all along.

I've known him to spend days trying to remember or find out somebody's name because he knew that they knew somebody he wanted to get to do something, and he figured that if they approached the real target it would be better than if he had to do it his self, and risk not being able to get everything all lined up like he likes.

I've heard some people fussing and cussing about the way he does things, but I'll say this: it's worked so far.

A few years back, what is now Kingsport was a kind of swamp land that nobody in their right mind would have wanted to own. And every time Jay Fred pulls off one of his schemes and gets something else here, the land values climb up a little bit higher, and a few more folks move in, and the stores do a little more business, and so do the other kinds of firms, and Jay Fred puts some more money into the pockets of the rich men who own the   Improvement Company, and now and   then- maybe a dollar or two in his own   pocket.

As nearly as I could figure out from what he said, Jay Fred wanted to get in touch with Woods at the real estate firm in New York, in order to find out something about somebody that might be interested in putting up money to build a hospital here. I never seen such a man for making deals in my life!

Anyway, he seemed mighty pleased over having found out the man's name he had been trying to   think of, and the name of the real estate company and all, so he told me a little more about his idea.

He said there was a certain organization that he had heard of that would put money into things like that, and then let the local folks put up money as well, and raise a whole lot of cash, and be a community service and a community hospital for the people and all and that if he could get to the right people, he thought he might be able to work something out, and that he was pretty sure that Woods had some connections with the people he wanted to get to talk to.

We talked about it some. Jay Fred knows that I don't talk about things like that to everybody in town,   because I know there are times a man is supposed to keep his mouth shut. I know I am telling a lot now, but that's different, because it has all already happened and is over with, and it couldn't make no difference to anybody one way or another now, but right at the time, I knew how to keep my own counsel, and that's what I did.

"But, Jay Fred, how do they come out?" I asked him, knowing blamed well that nobody gives you something for nothing. "How do they make money out of giving money away?"

He smiled at that. And he kind of talked in riddles for a while. Although he never did just come out and tell me, I sort of got the idea that it was a long-term sort of thing that his backer, whoever they might be, would consider an investment.

Although the hospital would be called a "community" hospital and all, and the people who donated money and part of their pay to build it would think they owned it, that wouldn't be the real way it was, and the money boys would keep their hand in just enough to siphon off a little here and a little there over the years, and it would be good for all concerned, especially in the long run. Besides, the local money that would be raised would go back to the folks who put up the big money to start with, if it was more than was really needed, and, it probably would be, because all the plants and businesses would get behind the drive and put pressure on their workers to give a share of their pay, which they would because they would think they were getting something for it, and in a way, maybe they would be at that.

"But it is still a good deal, Pug," he told me. "They get what they want, and we get what we want, which is a new hospital for our community."

Of course, you could have took that at least two ways, and may be even more. If you looked at it one way, what Jay Fred had in mind would bring a hospital to town, which we needed, he said, and that would be a fine thing for the community, I guess, for there are always sick people, it seems.

Looking at it the other way, if I understood it right, what might be going to happen was that Jay Fred and his friends was going to get some rich people to put up money to build a hospital, and then they was going to get local folks to give money to build the hospital, and give that money back to the fellers they got the money from in the first place, except they would keep on giving them a little money now and then along, just as long as the hospital kept operating, and they would claim it was a "community" hospital that the people owned, but the people never would really own it, and some day, if they ever wanted to, they might up and throw the "community" right out of it and just have it as a private business that was bought and paid for out of money that folks give, but surely they wouldn't actually ever do nothing like that. Why, folks were likely to get awful mad over such a thing if it ever happened!

I guess a person can find something good and something bad in almost anything if he looks at it long enough and hard enough.

Personally, it didn't make a whole lot of difference to me. The only time I think about a hospital is if I need one, which I never have so far, and if I do, I don't care who owns it, just as long as they can treat me or care for me, or do whatever has to be done and get me well again so I can get as far away from it as possible.

There are people who like to be sick. If they haven't got something wrong with them, they worry about that so much they get a case of nerves, and that makes them sort of sick, so then they can be happy and quit worrying about it and enjoy a lingering illness.

Like old Mrs. Rafferty who used to live down on Sullivan Street. She kept telling people how bad her health was and how she was at the point of death's door for 97 years before they finally put her away. She outlived her husband and all six of her kids, all of her neighbors, and friends, relatives and more family cats than could be counted, mostly because she pretended she was so sick all the time that everybody else had to do her work for her and she got so rested up it took her a long time to get busy enough to use up any energy so she could die of old age.

It was a lot colder the next morning, because we had one of them what they call "Easter snaps" and the temperature dropped back down to nearly freezing.

For several days, we had been enjoying a beautiful spring, with the warmest part of the day getting well up into the seventies. Flowers were blooming all around, but I had noticed that the redbuds' color was showing just a little as I drove in from Blountville the day before, and I had been expecting it.

It didn't freeze, thank goodness, so the early tomatoes would still be alright, but it was cool enough to where you could see your breath, in a kind of fog-like smoke, if you blew hard into the air.

I was up early, had breakfast at a place on Sullivan Street where they serve bacon and eggs and call it "Adam and Eve on a raft," which I think is kind of silly, but it tastes all right anyway, especially since they throw in a serving of hashbrowns, toast, butter, jelly, and coffee.

In season, they'll even give you a big slice of tomato at no extra charge, but that's been out for some months now and won't come back in vogue until the garden truck gets ripe again.

I shelled out fifteen cents for my breakfast, went back outside and climbed into my car, and headed for the Blountville Courthouse.

There wasn't much traffic, just a log truck coming in, heading for the Mead, I'd guess, and another truck loaded with chickens. I don't know where the chickens were going. From the looks of the truck, they had already been some distance, and had more to go. Probably headed toward Knoxville, I thought. There's a plenty big market for chickens down there, because a couple of meat packing companies are located there and they buy hens to dress and sell.

It has always seemed a bit strange to me that you call it dressing a chicken when you kill it, gut it, pluck all the feathers off, and chop off its feet and head. Actually, a dressed chicken is about as far from being dressed as anything could be, but I suppose folks would feel funny calling them naked chickens, which they are, instead of dressed chickens, which they are not.

As the truck went past, heading the opposite direction from the way I was going, I thought to myself that I'd bet that Kinnie Wagner

71

would like to be on it, heading away from this town and this trial, even if he had to ride back there with the hens. But maybe not. The hens seemed headed for just as sudden and untimely an end as he might be getting, if they found him guilty, which it was beginning to look to me like they very probably would, no matter what the testimony in the trial amounted to.

They've sure improved the road to Blountville, and they plan to do even more, they say.

Back about a year ago, they starting fixing it, putting new bridges in where the old wooden plank bridges were getting worn out, widening the road in a few places so you can turn a car around without having to back up for miles, like you used to have to do, and even cutting into the banks at some of the sharper curves to give you a little more room to get around them in.

The new bridges are concrete, too. They'll probably last a thousand years, the road commissioner said. And they made them plenty wide enough so you can even get a car past a hay wagon on one of them! That's what they call progress, I guess. Jay Fred and some of the other businessmen say it is.

They like to see such things as road work done, and are always bragging about it when it is being done and complaining about how much it is needed if it is not being done.

It's pretty smart, it seems to me, to build roads and bridges out of concrete so they will last forever. Why, they'll probably never have to build another bridge on that road after they get them all finished. Now, if they'd concrete the roads, too, like Jay Fred keeps trying to get them to do, we'd be fixed up Jake for life, you might say. And it wouldn't never have to be done again, either, which is the best part of all.

I read in a book one time about the old Romans and how they built roads that are still being used, even after nearly 2,000 years, and how they are just about as good today as they were when they first built them. That, it seems to me, is the way the government ought to do things and I don't care if you are talking about the federal government, or the state, or even the county here. Do one thing at a time, do it right, and then move on to something else. That way, you'd not ever have to be always fixing and repairing and going back and doing little bits and pieces of work on everything, and each time you got finished with something, you'd know it was done forever and good.

As I drove along, I thought to myself how lucky we were that our county squires were going about it that way.

Why, the folks who live here fifty years from now can be happy that our county, here in 1925, was foresighted enough to build roads and bridges and things good enough so they'd never have to worry about them. They have been talking about building new school buildings, too. There are plenty of schools around the county, but they want to build big, fine brick buildings and close up the little ones they are using now. I heard them talking about what it was going to cost to build the new schools one day when I was at County Court, and it's a blamed good thing the building will be brick and last forever, because it will take most of that time to get the money's worth out of them, if the figures I heard were correct.

I didn't have any trouble finding a place to park this morning, because I seemed to have beat the crowd to the courthouse.

I was careful to park alongside the road, well back from the courthouse and the judge's private space, but where I could make sure that I could pull out anytime I wanted to, because nobody could block me in unless they just left their car right in the roadway.

Before I left Kingsport, I had picked up a copy of the newspaper, and I read it in the courtroom, in the same front row seat I had been taking.

There wasn't much in the newspaper that I didn't already know about. They had a report on that murder and suicide over near Gate City, just the way that Roy Pyle had told me. Of course, it would be the same because they got their story from him, and he told me the same thing that he told them. But there wasn't anything new printed about it. When the paper comes out this evening, there might be more about it.

Kingsport has an evening paper. Both Johnson City and Bristol have morning papers, like most of the big towns do. But the fellers who own the Times are smart enough to know that they can copy news out of the morning papers, so long as they are evening, and probably won't too many folks notice anyhow. Besides that, it keeps them from having to work nights, like they would have to do if they printed all the news in the early mornings, and that saves some on the payroll, because these pressmen are getting so uppity they demand an extra 52 cents a shift if they work nights instead of days.

It wasn't long before other people began to drift in and take seats in the courtroom. And by the time court convened, the place was packed as usual. I could see crowds of folks out in the halls when the doors opened, and I believe that about every seat was taken again. The fat lady who had been sitting beside me was either late or wasn't coming today, because she never showed up.

I didn't really miss her, but Preacher Mooney came over and sat down in the seat she had been using, and although he is a nice enough man, he has the bad habit of saying "Amen" under his breath all the time and it kind of gets on your nerves.

"This court is now in session," the bailiff declared.

"Amen!" said Preacher Mooney.

I could tell right then it was going to be a long, long day.

They got right into it.

The first witness today was Mrs. John F. Smith, widow of the slain officer. She took the stand with a crying baby in her arms.

Sympathetic eyes gazed on the grieving woman from all over the courtroom. I kind of thought it was a shame to have made her come to the trial and testify, but maybe she felt better by doing it.

Mrs. Smith's testimony concerned her dead husband's wound. His shirt, coat and undershirt were all displayed, each showing a hole in the left shoulder, which, said the prosecutor, was a bullet hole.

It was brief, and the defense attorneys didn't even ask for cross-examination.

I noticed then that Wright Cox, a lawyer from Gate City, Virginia, was seated at the defense table with Burrow, Warren and Wagner. I hadn't noticed him before, and I was sure he hadn't been there the day before.

It later developed that he had volunteered to come and help with the defense, being a friend of the Wagner family, but had been busy with another matter and unable to get there at the start, so he had come on when he found the time, like a good neighbor might be expected to do.

The prosecution's next witness was J. E. Bachelder, who said he was a photographer in Kingsport, and that he had made some pictures of the scene following the shooting, and he got them out and showed them to the court, and they took seven of them as evidence, and let him come down.

Two witnesses followed him, W.G. Pratt, and Mrs. E. S. Williams, and they both testified that a telephone call had been put in prior to the shooting relative to a disturbance on the river bank. The two of them told the same story, in the same words, and with almost the same expressions on their faces.

It was just my opinion, of course, but I figured that they had rehearsed their testimony together, sort of like learning a part in a school play. I don't mean to say that I thought they were not telling the truth, as they saw it, but blamed if somebody hadn't been making the two of them practice what they would say to be sure they got it down just right, and that always makes testimony sound fishy to me.

The next witness called was J. M. Hamlett, the undertaker.

He had been in Kingsport for sometime, burying people for Jay Fred. What I mean is that Hamlett runs the undertaking and casket department of Jay Fred's Commissary, or the "Big Store," as some folks call it. But the "Big Store" has been getting brokeup, and Jay Fred has been selling off different parts of it. He sold the hardware part to Flem Dobyns and George Taylor, and a while back he sold the undertaking and casket department to Hamlett. So Jimmy Dobson bought in with Hamlett and is now helping him undertake and bury folks. They call themselves Hamlett-Dobson Funeral Home.

Jimmy Dobson has been selling for Jay Fred for sometime, everything from suits to soup beans, over at the Big Store, and he is now studying under Hamlett to undertake. Hamlett was asked about Officer Smith's wounds. He stated that there was a hole in the policeman's left breast and that it was evidently caused by a pistol bullet.

He said he believed the bullet lodged near the victim's heart. The defense attorneys got up and asked did he know that for a fact, and he said, no, he didn't, because he didn't cut the bullet out or nothing like that, but from the way the wound looked, that is what he figured had happened, so they let him go without more questions.

Several members of Wagners family were seated on the front row with me today. The accused man's father, Charles Wagner, of Speers Ferry, Va., was seated almost directly behind his son. Oscar and Kelsey Wagner, his brothers, flanked the older man. His sister, Ollie, is to be a witness, somebody told me, but another one of the girls was there, occupying the seat next to her brother.

While the Kinnie Wagner trial was causing so much excitement and interest around Kingsport, a lot of the rest of the country was focused on Kentucky, where a man named Floyd Collins had been trapped in a sand cave, just beyond reach of the workmen who were laboring around the clock to rescue him.

Collins died before they could dig him out. W. H. Hunt, the miner who was in charge of the rescue work, kept his men at the effort, and they finally brought Collins' body out of the ground a few minutes after eight o'clock on the morning of April 23, 1925, the same day Kinnie Wagner was to take the stand in his own defense.

The news went out on the radio and was later carried by about every newspaper in the country.

Hunt asked the crowds of spectators who were crowded near to pass by and take a look at Collins' body.

"I don't want anybody to go away and say we brought up chunks of rags," he declared.

According to the radio report I heard at noon that day, neither Lee nor Andrew Collins, the father and brother of the victim, were present at the cave when the body was taken out, although both of them had been there for days and nights on end while the frantic digging went on.

They took the body to Cave City, Kentucky, for embalmment prior to burial. And the crowds standing around the Sand Cave, where the explorer died, slacked off before long.

It's strange how a murder or shooting or a trapped person in desperate condition always draws a crowd.

I can see why some folks go; they want to help in some way if they can. But a lot of the people who show up have no intention or desire to be of any help to anyone about anything, they just want to see what is going on, share in the excitement, and be able to tell about it later, I guess.

During the days and nights that Collins was trapped, slowly breathing his last, in the sandstone cave, there was even more people going and coming at the scene than there was at Blountville for Wagner's trial! Some promoters made money out of it by selling drinks, doughnuts, pies and even souvenirs, while the injured man was dying a few yards away, buried under caved-in rock and dirt that was so unstable it shifted, slid, and grew with each touch of the rescuers' picks and shovels.

Right after the noon lunch hour, the prosecution rested its case against Kinnie Wagner.

Attorney General Lovette asked for a conviction and for the maximum penalty, which, of course, meant death in the electric chair.

Judge Chase called on the defense to present its case, and Lawyer Burrows immediately called Wagner himself to the stand!

The silence in the courtroom was startling as the 22-year-old desperado, as he was being called by the newspapers, calmly placed his hand on the Bible, was sworn in, and took the witness stand.

Carefully guided through questions by Attorney Burrows, Wagner told his story in a clear, unhesitating voice. He made no show of emotion, other than holding his hands tightly clasped together during the testimony, and there was, perhaps, just a bit of strained eagerness as he answered the questions put to him. According to Wagner, on the morning of the shoot-out, he had left his cousin's home in Kingsport with Conley Henry in a truck, and they went up on Cherry Hill.

After that, he said, they drove down to the river, at the place the shooting was to occur a few hours later, near the railroad underpass.

Wagner said he asked Henry to go and get his 16 year old sister and bring her down to meet him there. He said Henry drove off and later returned with his sister and two other girls. They had been sitting near the river bank talking, Wagner said, for "about 10 to 30 minutes" when he happened to glance up and look across the field.

He saw an officer in uniform coming across the field, he said. The other members of the group saw the policeman then, he said, and one of them told him to "go!"

Young Wagner said he got up and slipped down the bank onto a path leading up the river. Bending low and walking fast, he hurried along the river bank path about 30 yards, and slipped near the edge of the river.

Wagner said he intended to swim across the river and get away, if possible, without having any trouble. At the water's edge, he paused for a minute and gazed over the cold, rushing stream. The current did not look too swift, he felt, and the wet discomfort of soaking clothes would be worth bearing if he could avoid a confrontation with the officer.

Wagner admitted that he was armed, and indicated that he intended to leave his gun, shoes, and sweater on the bank for his friends to retrieve while he made his swim across the treacherous waters.

But before he could put his thoughts into actions, Wagner said, a shot rang out from up the river, and he felt the breeze of a bullet as it cut through the air near his ear.

Wagner said he instinctively dodged to one side, ducking down a little at the sound of the shot. Before he could even straighten up, a second shot was fired, he said, this one also a narrow miss.

Without even thinking, Wagner said, he drew his gun and wheeled in the direction the shots came from. He swore he saw an officer with a gun in his hand, pointing and ready to shoot.

Wagner snapped off a shot at the officer but shots were by then being fired at him from down the river. He said he wheeled in that direction, saw an officer with his hand on his gun, apparently trying to pull it loose from its holster, and fired off a shot at him.

The officer fell, he said, and he then heard a noise on the bank above him and looked up that way, where he saw a man, with gun already drawn, aiming at him, so he shot that man as well and saw him fall.   By this time, some 20 to 50 shots had been fired. Wagner was unscratched, but at least three of those who had been shooting at him were on the ground.

Wagner testified that he looked back down the river and saw a man, still holding a pistol in his hand, running away.

"I could have killed him easily," the young desperado said, "but I didn't want to."

I happened to be sitting alongside of the wall in front where Deputy Sheriff Joe Groseclose was standing, just at that time.

His face was red again, and his eyes were focused on the floor in the front of him, trying to bore a hole right through the oaken planks.

I looked back up at the witness and realized that young Wagner was staring directly at Groseclose, a faint smile on his lips.

It was evident that the Deputy Sheriff would not meet his eyes.

During that part of his testimony, I believe you could have heard a pin drop anywhere in the courtroom. People were actually straining to hear each word.

Why, I wondered, would the officers come up on Wagner with their guns already drawn, if they didn't know it was him and did not intend to shoot if possible?

And, if he was telling the truth, why would they start shooting, even before they called out to him to surrender?

Up until that point, I had personally figured that the officers had been telling the straight of it, and that they had gone down there not knowing that Wagner was anywhere around, to investigate a disturbance, like they had sworn to in court.

But it didn't seem right to me that they would walk up and start shooting, just on a disturbance investigation.

Wagner went on to tell how he had walked away from the scene of the shooting, taken a horse away from a young man who came riding along, and made his escape.

His story fit the testimony that D. R. Poe had given earlier, but with more details.

He told how he rode up Cherry Hill and over the ridge, and how he swam the horse across the river and then let it go, so it could find its way back home.

Wagner said he then went on foot until he got to Waycross, where he had spent the night, and give himself up in the morning.

Attorney General Lovette cross-examined, obviously trying to trap Wagner up with hard questions. Under his grilling, Wagner told how he had traveled with a "Wild West Show," or circus, in which he rode broncos, and admitted that he had been carrying pistols for about six months.

He denied, however, that he had been a sharp-shooter with the circus, which seemed to come as a kind of surprise to most of the folks in the courtroom.

From all the talk and publicity about him so far, most everybody thought he was a kind of male Annie Oakley, making his living as a circus trick-shot, which he was now saying wasn't so.

Young Wagner also admitted that he had killed a man in Mississippi with a shotgun and that he was wanted in that state on a charge of murder.

He said he came to his aunt's home in Hawkins County in December or January and since that time had been in Hawkins County, or Scott County, Virginia, or Gate City, or about Kingsport.

He admitted, under the rapid-fire cross-examination, that he came into Kingsport and spent two days and one night there before the shooting took place.

Wagner also said he knew of the reward that had been offered for him in Mississippi, and that he had provided himself with pistols, which I would guess almost anybody would want to do if they figured the "dead or alive" business on the reward offer meant what it said, which it did.

I don't understand how the law can offer a thousand-dollar reward, put up by individuals, for vengeance, if it takes breaking the law to collect it. It looks to me like it would be just as much against the law to kill a man who was wanted for killing a man, so's you could get a reward that was offered for him, as it would be against killing a man in the first place so somebody could offer a reward for somebody else to kill you, but it gets kind of confusing when you think about it, and maybe that's how they got away with doing it.

When court convened the next morning at 8:40, Wagner was smiling as he came into the courtroom with Sheriff Joe Thomas and took his seat with his attorneys.

D. R. Poe was the first witness to take the stand that day, and he told of how, on the morning of April 14, Wagner gave himself up to him (Poe) at his store in Waycross, Virginia, admitting that he had "killed two men and probably three" in Kingsport.

"He said he had killed them in self-defense and wasn't sorry for it," Poe testified.

Poe said that Wagner wanted him to promise that he would give his sister half of the reward which was out for his capture and did not want any officer to take him, but would rather give up to a disinterested citizen.

The defense scored on cross-examination when Poe declared that Wagner told him that he had been surrounded by officers in Kingsport and that he had shot in self-defense.

Poe admitted, however, that he was afraid to try to get Wagner's second gun from him after the desperado had given him one gun.

Deputy Sheriff Joe Groseclose was called back to the stand briefly to testify concerning the guns found on the dead officers.

The next witness to take the stand was Conley Henry, who testified that he took Wagner to the scene at which the tragedy occurred, and that at Wagner's request, he later brought the gunman's sister and two other girls to the spot near the river bank.

Henry said he was talking to two of the girls when he heard two or three shots fired from up the river in the direction in which Wagner in the meantime had gone.

He said that Officers Smith and Groseclose came by and that Smith asked him what the shooting was about.

He stated that after the officers passed him, he heard another shot and saw Smith sink to the ground. He told of Wagner's escape on horseback after the shooting.

When asked on cross-examination if he hadn't told an officer that Wagner was on the river, he stubbornly denied that he had.

Another material witness for the prosecution was Andy Herron, who testified that he came down near the river with Officers Miller and Frazier, and that someone further down the river fired a shot and that he saw Frazier fall.

According to his testimony, neither of the officers had fired prior to this shot.

He swore that Miller ran toward him about 15 steps when the first shot was fired, then ran up on the bank and fired at the man who had shot Frazier.

Herron admitted, however, that he himself ran when the shooting commenced.

The state introduced several other witnesses in building up its network of evidence, among them Deputy Sheriffs John H. Parrott and S. N. Light, by whose testimony the state attempted to show that it would have been impossible for the officers to shoot each other.

I figured that was a waste of time, and just showmanship on the part of the prosecuting attorneys, because Wagner had already admitted that he shot the officers, and whether or not they could have shot each other didn't have a blamed thing to do with it, as far as I could see.

There came close to being a real hassle when the state put Sheriff W. J. Turner of Greene County, Mississippi, on the stand and started introducing evidence to show that Wagner had killed a man in that state, and that a reward of $1,000 was offered for the capture of the man committing the crime. The defense attorneys all jumped to their feet and started objecting right and left.

Judge Guy S. Chase finally agreed to allow the state to introduce the testimony, but would not allow the attorneys to go into detail relative to it, which didn't make no sense to me neither, but that's what he done.

L. E. Bellamy, probation officer of Scott County, Va., was then called as a witness for the prosecution. He swore that he was in the police headquarters in Kingsport at about 3:30 o'clock in the afternoon on the day of the shooting when a telephone call was received, by reason of which the five officers went off in a car.

Lawyer Burrows, the defense attorney from Bristol, asked him if he heard what was said over the telephone and Bellamy said he did, that the officer who had taken the call had told him.

Burrows said did he actually hear the voice over the telephone wire, and Bellamy admitted that he hadn't.

Burrows said it was hearsay, then, wasn't it, because he hadn't actually heard the voice on the telephone and all he knew was what somebody said was said, and Bellamy said he reckoned that was right, and Burrows just looked at the judge and kind of shook his head and sat down and said he didn't have no more questions for that witness.

I saved newspaper clippings of the trial, and a lot about what happened. They told it pretty well, I think. For instance, the remainder of that day's court proceedings was reported as follows:

"Wagner remained cool throughout the examination of the other witnesses, and the immense crowd was absolutely quiet, with much interest being manifested in the case throughout the day.

"Through the testimony introduced during the latter part of the afternoon, the counsel for the state continued to weave the scheme of evidence which it believes is dragging the prisoner to his doom. Slowly but surely, as the long hours drag through the afternoon, the Commonwealth built up its case, with the defense attorneys stubbornly fighting every inch of the ground.

"Throughout the latter part of the afternoon session, several more officers, policemen and deputy sheriffs were called to the stand, their testimony collaborating in the main the evidence presented by other officers who had testified earlier in the day.

"Sheriff S. N. Light testified that following the tragedy on April 13, he had talked with Wagner at the jail about the shooting.

"He said that Wagner told him that he had shot Frazier up the river then Smith down the river, and then "the fellow" came up over the bank on him, and he shot him.

"He said he thought they were going to mob him and that was the only way out, the deputy sheriff testified.

"Light stated that Wagner told him that Smith started for his gun just as he, Wagner, shot him.

"D. J. Heaberlin, Chief of Police of Bristol, Tennessee, followed Deputy Sheriff Light on the stand.

"He too, swore that he had talked with the prisoner at the jail subsequent to the shooting.

"Wagner mentioned his belt, Chief Heaberlin testified.

"He told Chief Thomas that he would like to wear it until it was all over and that he could keep it as a souvenir.

"He swore that when he questioned Wagner about the shooting, the prisoner told him that he had killed an officer in Mississippi and that there was a thousand dollar reward out for him ... that he saw five officers coming around him, thought they were going to arrest him and take him back to Mississippi.

"He stated, according to Heaberlin's testimony, that he didn't want them to arrest him, and that is why he killed them."

According to Heaberlin's testimony, Wagner stated that he shot three of the five officers, one ran, and the other got behind a tree.

C. L. Maines, officer of Bristol, Tennessee Police Force, followed his chief on the stand.

Maines, like Light and Heaberlin, testified that he had talked with Wagner relative to the case in the Blountville jail subsequently to the shooting.

"He said he had done the wrong thing, but that they were after him and he thought he would get them before they got him," Maines swore.

Little was brought out in the cross-examination of these officers, which was, in itself, brief.

The most material witness introduced during the afternoon was Mrs. W. H. Rhodes, a widow of near Waycross, Virginia, and near whose home the confessed slayer gave himself up.

She swore that shortly after 11 o'clock on the night of the fateful tragedy, Wagner, evidently pretty near exhausted and a fugitive from justice, came to her home and talked to her through a window.

Wagner told her at that time, she said, that he wanted to get a pencil and some paper, as he wished to write his people, declaring that he was going to kill himself.

"He said that he had done some dirt," Mrs. Rhodes swore.

She testified that he later said, "Oh, Lord, what will I do?" and that she told him to trust in the Lord. She stated that he spent the remainder of that night of the fated day in the haymow of her barn, and that the following morning, she found him in the hay and again talked with him.

She told him to surrender, she said on the stand, and that would give him a chance to save his soul, after he had told her the trouble he was in.

There was a tense stillness in the crowded courtroom when the aged widow added a final statement that brought tears to the eyes of many who heard her.

She told how she talked with Wagner, and said he told her of the trouble he was in, and that he had decided to kill himself, and wanted to write his people one last time.

She said he told her that he feared he had gone too far to ever be forgiven, and felt the best thing he could do was just end his life.

But, she said, she told him that the Lord would forgive him, if he sincerely asked, and that he still had a chance to "save his soul."

"I know my mother is in heaven," she said he told her. And, he said he wouldn't be afraid to die if he had to.

Mrs. Rhodes testified that while she was talking to Wagner, Neil Bussell came up and told Wagner that he had heard that he, Wagner, had killed six men over at Kingsport.

Wagner replied, she said, that he had only killed two men... and maybe three.

Right after that, when the defense attorneys were cross-examining Mrs. Rhodes, the lawyers got into a squabble that I thought was going to end up in a fistfight, they all seemed to get so mad about it.

Attorney Warren asked to introduce as evidence a note, which he said Wagner had written at the Rhodes home, in Mrs. Rhodes' presence.

It was on a little piece of paper, and I finally figured out that it was on the back of a blank check. Bandy and Lovette and McAmis all jumped up and starting objecting, and the other prosecution attorneys grabbed law books and starting searching through them, trying, I suppose, to find a law that would be against receiving the evidence.

For a time, they went at it hard and heavy.

Judge Guy S. Chase finally permitted the note to be entered as evidence and read.

Scribbled in pencil on ... I was right ... the back of a blank check, it was the note the young desperado had written to his little sister while believing he was at the point of death, a hunted, desperate man, who knew he was worth far more dead than alive due to a thousand dollar reward on his head.

"Dear Sister," it said, "believe they will get me so I will fix things up so you will go through school." That was all. No signature, no further explanation.

But it kind of made you think.

Here was this young man, accused of being a wild, vicious, ruthless killer .. and his thoughts, while at the point of ending his life in desperation, were apparently fixed on the future welfare of a kid sister he was going to have to leave behind.

Several expert witnesses were called to the stand in that afternoon session. Dr. O. S. Hauk, a Kingsport physician, testified early in the afternoon relative to the wound which caused Officer Smith's death.

The Town of Gate City, Virginia, as it looks today. Scott County's most famous "outlaw", Kinnie Wagner, is still talked about when ole timers get together.

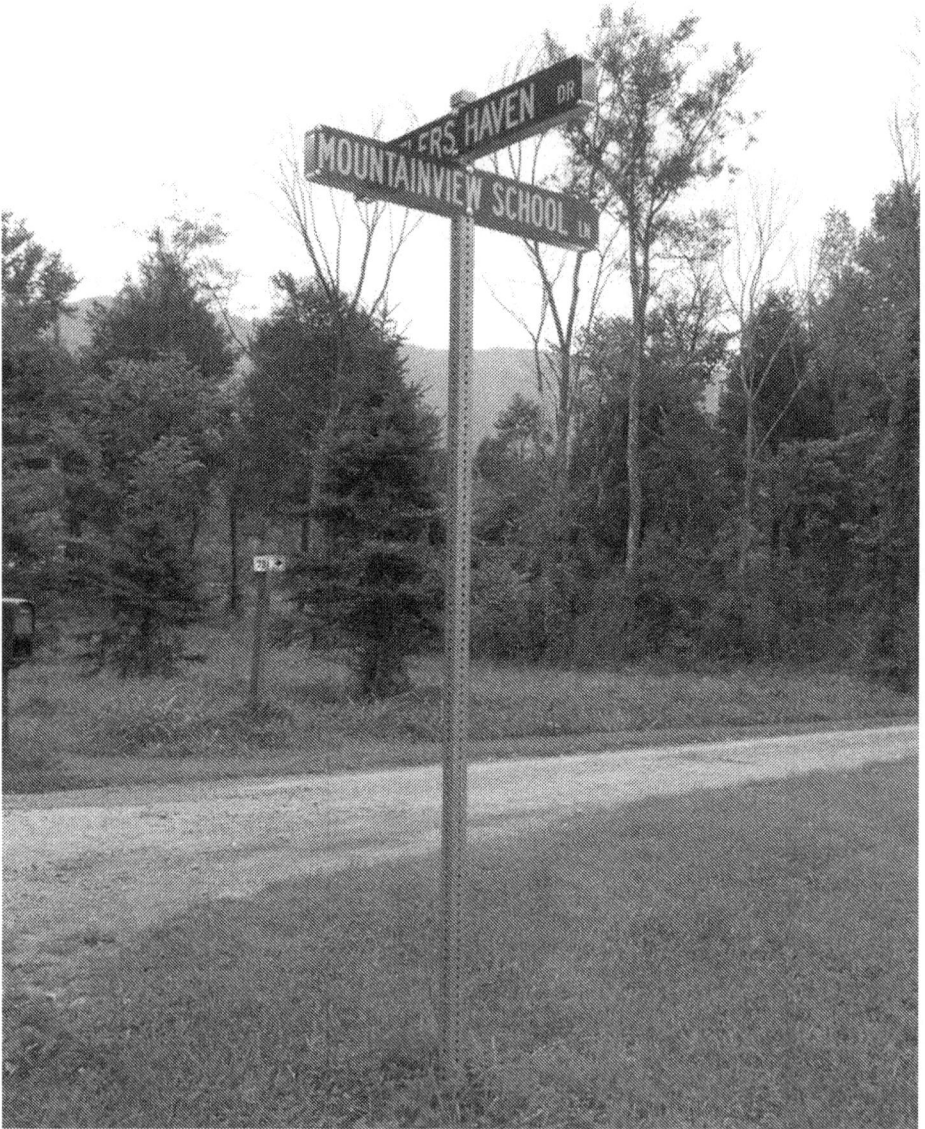

To find Kinnie Wagner's grave, visitors to Scott County should take the road to Nickelsville and then turn on "Rattlers Haven Road. The take Mountainview School Road to the former Mountview School building, now a private residence. The cemetery is just beyond. This photo shows the street sign just off the road to Nickelsville.

The old Mountainview School building. Kinnie Wagner is buried in the cemetery behind and to the right of the structure, which is now a private residence.

Just beyond the old Mountainview School building, is the fenced in old graveyard. Kinnie Wagner's grave is to the left of center in this photo.

A single marker – no headstone – marks the final resting place of Scott County's most notorious outlaw, Kinnie Wagner. Many of the other graves in the cemetery are a distance apart from the Wagner burial site.

Kinnie Wagner's grave at the old Mountainview School cemetery, just outside Gate City, VA on the road to Nickelsville.

The Holston River as it looks today, the scene of the famous shoot-out with Kinnie Wagner.

The riverbank where the famous shoot-out with Kinnie Wagner took place is now a city park with a paved walkway, picnic tables and children's playground area.

The old Kingsport Hospital, where many of the wounded were taken following the famous shoot-out with Kinnie Wagner still stands on Netherland Inn Road. The structure is now an apartment complex.

He stated that the bullet entered the officer's left breast and remained in the body.

Death was caused, he said, by the bullets severing one of the main arteries leading from the heart.

D. Beck, a civil engineer of Kingsport, who made blueprints of the scene of the shooting following the tragedy, was called to the stand to testify relative to these blueprints. One of the blueprints was introduced before the court as an exhibit and was placed before the jury while the engineer explained from it the positions of the several "actors in the drama," as these positions had been designated to him.

Neil Bussell, one of the two men to whom Wagner gave himself up on the morning following the tragedy, told of the events transpiring on that morning.

Bussell testified that after the youthful slayer had given himself up to him and Poe, he had asked them to take him to the officers at Gate City, and he, Bussell, told Wagner to give one of his pistols to Poe and to keep the other himself to protect them, as he feared a mob...

"I killed two men in Kingsport yesterday and shot another," Bussell quoted the young cowboy-killer as saying.

Bussell stated that he, Poe and Wagner were on their way to Gate City to turn the latter over to officers there when their car was smashed into by a car containing several Sullivan County officers, the collision evidently being accidental, according to Bussell.

The latter went on to tell about how he and Poe were relieved of their prisoner by these officers.

He said that after the collision, he and Poe had started on up the road to Gate City on foot, with their prisoner, when Deputy Sheriff Clark stopped them and demanded that Wagner be turned over to him, declaring that he "had papers" for him.

Bussell testified that in spite of his remonstrations, the officers then took the prisoner off with them. The defense scored a point when Bussell admitted on cross-examination that Wagner told him he had killed a man in Kingsport to protect himself.

"Deputy Sheriff J. R. Fulk, one of the officers who had relieved Poe and Bussell of the prisoner on the road to Gate City, was the next witness to take the stand," the clipping continued.

"Fulk said that he was driving the car which wrecked with the car of Poe and Bussell, and that he purposely drove into the car when he recognized one of the passengers in it as a man corresponding to the description of Wagner.

94

"He testified that he and Deputy Clark took a gun off of Wagner, and that they then brought him, by way of Kingsport, to Blountville.

"Fulk quoted Wagner as saying that he had fired four shots in the pistol battle at Kingsport, and that he believed that he got two men.

"Yesterday afternoon's session was adjourned by Judge Chase at 5:15."

The next day, April 24, 1925, presented another interesting newspaper account:

"Jury To Get Wagner Case This Afternoon," the headline screamed.

"6 Hours Set As Time Of Arguments By Councils."

"Fate Of Wagner May Be Given To Jury By 6 p.m."

"Each Side Given 3 Hours To Argue Case"

"Verdict Is Not Expected Before Court Convenes Early Tomorrow"

"Jury Appears Weary After Long Days Of Strenuous Duty - While Wagner Seems Somewhat Jaded and Tired—Largest Crowd of Any Time at Trial Present at Blountville Today."

"The fate of youthful Kinnie Wagner, on trial for his life at Blountville for the alleged murder of Policeman John F. Smith, will be given into the hands of the jury late this afternoon, probably between 5 and 6 o'clock.

"It is unlikely that a verdict will be returned before the convening of court early tomorrow morning. Both the state and the defense finally rested the case at 9:50 o'clock this morning, after taking the testimony of several rebuttal witnesses by the prosecution, and the arguments of the case proper began promptly at 10:05 a.m.

"The members of the jury appeared weary this afternoon, and, after the strain of the past four days, the prisoner himself appeared to be somewhat jaded and tired, though he maintained his attitude of perfect calm and composure."

"Throughout the day, he sat as usual by the side of his counsel, with some of his friends and relatives near him.

"He was attired the same as on the previous day of the trial, save that he was wearing a woolen shirt.

"By agreement, the time set for the arguments of the case was 6 hours, 3 hours for the state and 3 hours for the defense.

"The arguments being begun at 10:05 a.m, it will thus be completed by 5:05 o'clock this afternoon.

"About 45 minutes will be required for Judge Guy S. Chase to charge the jury, and then the fate of the 22-year-old desperado will rest in the hands of 12 jurymen".

"It is not regarded as likely, however, that the court will hold for decision this afternoon.

"The first speaker for the prosecution this morning was Luke M. McAmis, of Kingsport, for prosecution, who spoke from 10:05 until 10:20 a.m.

"He was followed by Lyle Burrow, of Bristol, for the defense, who spoke from 10:20 until 11 a.m.

"T. R. Bandy, of Kingsport, for the prosecution, who spoke from 11 a.m. to 11:40 a.m., being followed by Wright Cox, of Gate City for the defense, who spoke from 11:40 until 12:30 p.m.

"The court adjourned at 12:30 until 1:30 in the afternoon. The first speaker after the lunch hour was James R. Worley of Kingsport, for the prosecution, followed in the arguments of the case by George M. Warren, of Bristol, for the defense.

"Attorney General O. B. Lovette, for the prosecution, was on the stand when this newspaper went to press this afternoon..."

It got kind of confusing, I thought.

Listening to the lawyers for the prosecution, I got to feeling that the Wagner boy was a dangerous, ruthless, quick-acting killer who needed to be put away or locked up to keep him from shooting just anybody who happened along.

But then one of the lawyers for the defense would get up and I would get to listening to what he said, and before I realized it, I was thinking the police had done Wagner wrong, by going down there to kill him if they could, so they could get that thousand dollar reward, and he had just acted in self-defense to keep them from doing it.

The jury was having the same trouble, I could tell.

When the prosecutors got up and started talking, the jury members would sort of nod their heads in agreement after each strong charge or accusation.

Some of the prosecutor-lawyers, McAmis for one, I think, and Bandy for another, if I remember rightly...talked about the poor widow, left to raise her four children alone, due to Wagner's deadly shot killing her husband. They poured it on pretty thick, and I really got to feeling bad about it and sorry for her and all.

But then one of the defense lawyers, Warren, I think it was, told about how the policemen came running over the embankment,

96

shooting to kill, in hopes of splitting that reward money, and what else could Wagner do but shoot back?

The folks crowded into the courtroom were split over it, too. About half of them were all for sending Wagner to the electric chair, and the other half would rather see a medal pinned on him.

Here's what the papers said that day:

"The courtroom was crowded throughout the day today with the crowd at the little county seat much larger today than it had been either of the previous days of the trial.

"In spite of the stifling heat, the courthouse was crowded even to the halls and outside entrances, with many people standing on the streets anxiously awaiting the outcome of the trial.

"With the convening of court this morning, several rebuttal witnesses were introduced by the state, among them Chief Cam A. King of the local police force and Deputy Sheriffs John H. Parrot and S. N. Light.

"The purpose of the state in introducing these witnesses was to refute the testimony given yesterday afternoon by Miss Hagar Brooks.

"Brooks, who testified that from the porch of her home, just below the tannery, she saw the gun battle and saw two officers go over the bank, firing as they went.

"Chief King stated that he had stepped off the distance from the Brooks home to the scene of the tragedy and found it to be 400 yards.

"Deputy Parrot stated that after Chief King had gone down on the river bank with several other men, he and Deputy Light stood on the porch of the Brooks home and were unable to distinguish from that distance which of the men were officers or which were in ordinary civilian clothes.

"He declared that he could not tell from that distance whether or not one of the men had on a policeman's uniform, and would have been unable to tell whether or not one of the men had anything in his hand.

"He admitted, however, on cross-examination that he was able to distinguish that the Chief had on a hat and not a cap.

"The testimony of Deputy Light was practically identical with that of Deputy Parrot."

That bothered me some. I never feel too confident about witnesses when they sound like they have got together and memorized their stories before they get up on the stand.

Why, it is dang near impossible for two different people to tell the same story of what they saw happen and tell it the same way. Sometimes, just the simplest thing you can think of gets all turned and twisted when two different folks try to tell about what they saw happen.

So when two law officers get up in court and swear the same thing, telling it the very same way, just like they have got it all written out in front of them and are reading it, I don't put a whole lot of confidence in it myself.

"Dewey Nelson, the star witness for the defense, was recalled to the stand for the brief period following the testimony of the officers and admitted, upon being questioned by the counsel for the defense, that he had been convicted in courts of Kingsport several times on the charge of fighting and drunkenness.

"Following the testimony of Nelson, both sides rested their cases.

"The defense rested its case at 5:30 o'clock yesterday afternoon with evidence of Andy King, whose testimony relative to the number of shots that were fired was brief and of little consequence.

"Only nine witnesses in all were introduced by the defense, including the prisoner himself, the attorneys for Wagner consuming only a half of a day for the introduction of their testimony, while the prosecution had consumed a day and a half.

"Kinnie Wagner himself remained on the stand for an hour and a half, about an hour of this time being taken up in a rigid, grueling, cross-examination to which he was subjected by Attorney General O. B. Lovette.

"The prisoner, was utterly calm, save for the slight nervousness manifested in the too-great eagerness with which he sometimes answered questions and the tightly clasped fingers gripped about his knee.

"He answered the questions directly and unhesitatingly. Only on one or two occasions did he appear to become slightly confused.

"He was followed on the stand by his sister, Ollie Wagner, a pretty 16-year old high school girl, who was talking with him at the quiet spot on the river bank, which later became a scene of carnage when the officers arrived on the fated afternoon of April 13.

"Miss Wagner answered the questions of the attorneys with the same directness which had characterized the testimony of her brother, but with even more coolness and deliberation.

"Her testimony for the most part collaborated the testimony given by her brother.

"She stated that he was the first of their party to see the approach of an officer and that immediately he became aware of the approach of the policemen and deputy sheriffs he attempted to escape toward the river.

"Amy Lou Penley, a second cousin of the Wagners and another member of the little gathering on the river on that fateful Monday, presented testimony which pretty largely bore out the testimony of her girlfriend, which was, in several salient features, contradictory to the testimony which had been given by Conley Henry, a witness for the state.

"She said that when Henry and the three girls set out in the truck to meet Kinnie Wagner on the river side, that Henry asked that either she or the Tipton girl set on the lap of Ollie Wagner, since he didn't want the officers to see her going down there."

Conley Henry had testified that he did not know that Wagner was a fugitive from justice with a heavy reward on his head, but the Penley girl's statement sure contradicted that.

Then the Penley girl testified that while they were seated on the river bank, Wagner first noticed the approach of the officers and exclaimed, "My Lord, there's an officer!"

He then ran over the bank toward the river, she said.

She stated that Officers Smith and Groseclose then passed the girls, Smith some distance in advance.

Just after they had paused, she said, Smith turned and motioned to Groseclose to come on up.

She said that the sounds of the first shots of the pistol battle came from further up the river, but she was unable to tell if this sound came from the spot which Kinnie Wagner had reached or from some place still further up the side of the stream.

The testimony of the Penley girl to the effect that Smith and Groseclose both passed them, with Smith a slight distance in the lead, was borne out by the testimony of Emma Tipton, the third girl of the little party by the river, who also swore that after the officers had passed, Smith motioned for Groseclose to come on up.

She stated that to the best of her judgment, about 20 or 25 shots were fired in all.

Hagar Brooks, a young girl who lives in a home by the side of the railroad, just below the tannery, testified that she witnessed a part of the tragedy from the front porch of her home, standing on a chair.

She said that she saw the officers divide forces near her home and approach the river at different points.

She stated that later, she saw one of the officers standing on the bank and that two others went over the bank, shooting as they went!

Upon later cross-examination, she testified that the latter two officers fired about ten shots before they went over the bank.

The star witness for the defense, with the exception of Wagner himself, was Dewey Nelson, the man upon whose horse Wagner escaped from Kingsport following the pistol battle.

Nelson gave testimony which was in direct contradiction to testimony given earlier in the trial by Deputy Sheriff Joe Groseclose.

The defense witness said that after the smoke of the battle had cleared away and Wagner had made his escape, he and Groseclose carried Frazier up from the brink of the river.

Then, he testified, Groseclose told him to go down and get Smith's guns.

He swore that Smith was lying stretched out on the ground with his arms spread out, and that one of the dead officer's pistols was lying within two inches of his right hand.

Nelson said that he picked up the gun, took the officer's other gun out of his hip pocket and took them to Groseclose.

He swore that the gun which he said was lying on the ground by the dead man's hand had mud on it, and he declared that there was mud on the ground at that spot.

He also testified that after Wagner had shot the officers, he came up to him and demanded that he give him his horse.

According to his testimony, Wagner became more insistent when he demurred, and cried, "I want that horse, I don't mean no foolishness!"

On direct examination, Nelson said nothing about Wagner drawing a gun on him, but said on cross-examination that the fugitive had poked a pistol in his side in making his demand that he be given the horse.

Deputy Sheriff Groseclose, called by the state in rebuttal immediately after the defense rested its case, flatly denied the story which Nelson had told relative to the dead policeman's guns.

He swore that he did not tell Nelson to get Smith's guns and denied that Nelson either picked up a pistol from the ground or took one from the person of the dead policeman. He maintained that he himself took both of Smith's guns and that both were in the dead man's holsters, under his uniform coat, which he swore was buttoned!

Court was adjourned for the day by Judge Guy B. Chase on the third day of the Wagner trial about 6 o'clock.

The crowd attending the trial on the third day was about the same as that in appearance on the second day, but not so large as the crowd on the first day.

When I got outside the courthouse that Friday evening, Joe Crum was waiting for me.

"Hey, Pug," he called, "I want to talk to you."

"Hello, Joe," I said, and walked over to where he was waiting. "What's up?"

"We missed a lot of money today," he said. "If you hadn't stopped that hamburger deal we was in, we could have made a killing. There wasn't nobody at all selling food today, to amount to anything, except for that feller with the wrapped sandwiches. So what I want to know is will you do it again tomorrow? I bet we can sell a thousand hamburgers easy, with the crowd that will be here."

"Joe, I don't think so," I told him. "I'm not interested in trying it again, because others are in it now. We made a few dollars and got out at the right time, and that's what I like to do. But I'm not going to try it again tomorrow."

"Well, if you've got your mind made up, do you care if I go ahead and do it? Instead of you being in it, I mean?"

"Joe, I don't care what you do," I told him.

"Get all the hamburgers to sell you want to, I won't compete with you or mind your using my idea. I just don't want to bother with it anymore, and I don't want to invest in it."

"Oh, that's alright," Joe beamed. "I got a feller who will put up the money if I do the selling. I wanted to ask you first, though, because you started it, and I didn't want you to think I was stealing your idea."

"You're welcome to it, Joe. Good Luck. I hope you do well."

Joe slapped me on the back and walked off. I turned toward my car but just happened to glance back toward the direction he had gone in, and there he was, leaning on the door of that blamed yellow Buick,

101

talking to the smart-aleck who owned it and who was setting in the driver's seat!

He must have paid off a fine or something to get it released, because the deputy I talked to told me Judge Chase was so mad over that car being parked in his space he was going to sell it at auction just as soon as he got the Wagner trial over with and had the time to fool with contempt citations.

I will admit, the thought had crossed my mind that I might put in a bid on the blamed thing, because I still had a kind of recurring hankering for it that was a cross between being envious of the driver because it was such a nice looking car and being mad at him because he was such a smart-aleck, but anyway, I had it.

Well, if he had got it out of the locked garage down behind the jail, he must have settled with Judge Chase, so I guessed he would just go on driving around town like a big shot and giving me a slow burn inside every time I saw him at it.

I didn't think no more about it and drove back home to Kingsport that April day wondering how long it would take the jury to decide whether to give Wagner a life sentence or send him to the electric chair, that new fangled death machine they installed at the state prison a while back. It was a foregone conclusion that they would find him guilty, I figured, because he admitted that he had done the killing.

If I was in the same fix, I might have done the same thing, I don't know. It's just in the movies, like with William S. Hart and fellers like that, where you just shoot a gun out of somebody's hand without hurting them too bad. But I'd guess that if a bunch of fellers came over the bank shooting, like that Brooks girl said she saw them do, a man would be entitled to shoot back.

Of course, the police told a different tale, but the Brooks girl sounded to me like she was telling the truth.

If I was Wagner, I figured I'd just sort of toss a coin between life in prison and the electric chair, and be willing to take whichever one came up, but having never been him or in a fix like he was in, I didn't reckon I was really qualified to make such a call. You never know what you'd do if you was in the same fix another feller is in, so it don't pay none too much to say you'd do this or you'd do that when you really don't know what you'd do, because you have not ever had to face the same thing he is facing.

It was a bright spring evening, and I enjoyed the cool air blowing in the windshield. That courthouse had been hot, with the windows all closed up like they were, and with so many people crowded inside.

I wondered for a while why they had the windows closed, and I had asked one of the deputies about it and he said that the judge had ordered it that way. The judge told him, that if the windows were open, so somebody could maybe see Wagner, if they got on top of a house nearby or someplace like that, or if they got up on a hill and used field glasses or a telescope, there was always a chance they might try to shoot him, and he sure wasn't going to let anything like that happen.

I didn't figure that anybody would go that far, but you never really know. Most of the folks I had talked to seemed to think that Wagner hadn't done anything that just about any other man would have done, if he could do it, except for the lawyers and the law who were prosecuting him.

But in the crowd that day, I had seen this dentist I know, sitting up near the front, taking it all in, and muttering under his breath against Wagner. I passed by him close enough one time to hear his whispered words, and he kept saying, "dirty killer, dirty killer!" over and over, like he was real mad, and would like to throw the switch on the electric chair current himself or something if he got the chance. I couldn't figure out what it was to him, but I found out more about that later.

I drove on home that evening, put my car in my rented garage, and walked back to the boarding house.

Some of the fellers who also boarded there were sitting out on the front porch, talking about the Wagner trial. When they saw me coming up the sidewalk, a couple of them jumped up and hollered at me, asking what the jury gave Kinnie Wagner.

"Are they sending him to the 'lectric chair," Mike Mosley asked, "or giving him life?"

"They haven't decided yet, so far as I know," I told him, explaining that the jury had just got the case.

"Boy, I'll bet you there will be a mob of people at Blountville tomorrow!" Jack Jenkins said. "That place will be so crowded you won't be able to stand up!"

I had been telling them about the trial and what had happened each day after I got in at night, and about how many people were there, and

103

other things like that, which you can't hardly get out of a newspaper story.

Jack worked over at the brick yard and he hadn't been able to get to the trial a single time, although he said he knew Kinnie Wagner personally, was a good, close friend of his, and had gone to school with him and played with him a lot when they were youngsters.

So many people told me things like that during the trial that I almost got to worrying about it. It seemed like I was the only feller in Kingsport who didn't know Kinnie Wagner personally, hadn't grown up as his best buddy, and was, therefore, entitled to share in the limelight by at least some reflected glory or notoriety, dim though it may have been.

It is funny how people always feel better if they can claim they know somebody who happens to be in the news, even bad news, just so long as they can claim they know somebody you don't know, and they kind of act like that gives them a special kind of knowledge about what is going on.

Personally, I have learned that I don't know even the people I do know …at least I don't know them well enough to figure out what they would do about something or why they would do it or want to do whatever they done in the first place, and in the second place, what difference could it make anyhow?

It was a little chillier that Saturday morning, cooler than it had been for some few days, but still with temperatures high enough to not bother the early fruit tree blossoms.

I didn't really have any reason to go to the last day of the trial, having seen and heard enough about it to do me well enough, but I had so much time already invested in it, I thought I might as well see the finish as well as the beginning. Besides, this feller I knew wanted me to go to Bristol for him to pick up a gear he was having made at the Bristol Foundry, and I figured that would be as good a day as any to do it.

The judge had said he was going to convene court early that morning, and he probably figured that since it was Saturday, most of them would like to get up and get it over with as soon as they could, so they could go about their regular weekend business.

Maybe it is just the way I look at it, but I've noticed that judges and such officials don't mind asking people to spend time on jury duty or other such obligations as long as it is workday time. But they seldom tie up working men on Saturdays or Sundays or holidays, which must mean that they figure that a man can spare time from work alright, but expecting him to take his non-working time for government duty is too much to expect from voters.

At any rate, I got to Blountville early and it was a good thing that I did, because Judge Chase convened court at 7:30.

Kinnie Wagner came into the courtroom holding onto the arm of Sheriff Joe Thomas. The prisoner was smiling, talking to Thomas in a friendly way as though they were joking about something.

Looking at the youthful defendant, you wouldn't think he had a care in the world!

I looked for the crowd to start coming in most any time, but there were only a handful of people in the courtroom.

The prosecution attorneys were at their table, and Wagner's attorneys were seated at the other one. Wagner smiled and spoke to his attorneys and sat down at the defense table.

Up on the bench, Judge Guy S. Chase shuffled through some papers for a minute or two, and then told the bailiff to bring the jury in.

As soon as they walked in the door, I could tell that they were tired. Somebody had told me just before court convened that the jury had deliberated for a little more than 13 hours, taking several votes before they reached a verdict. That meant that some of them had been for finding Wagner guilty and some of them must have been against it or they wouldn't have needed to take more than one vote.

They didn't go back into the jury box. Instead, they ranged themselves before the bench, facing Judge Chase.

"Gentlemen," his honor asked, "have you reached a verdict?"

"We have, your honor," the spokesman for the jury replied.

"What is your verdict?" Judge Chase asked.

The spokesman for the jury didn't turn around or even glance in Wagner's direction. He kept his eyes fixed on Judge Chase, as if there wasn't anyone else in the courtroom.

I looked at Wagner and saw that he was watching the spokesman closely, sitting very still, almost as if he was holding his breath. But he looked cool and calm, as though he was just waiting for a conversational reply to a question he had asked to someone.

"Your honor," the spokesman said, "we have found the prisoner guilty as charged, and recommend death by electrocution."

There was a moment of complete silence just after the jury spokesman announced the guilty verdict. Then, almost as if by signal, a low buzz of conversation began, as people started excitedly whispering to each other about it.

Judge Chase banged down his gavel and called for order and the sound stopped, just like he had thrown a switch.

Attorney Lyle Burrows was on his feet. "Your Honor," he said, "may I approach the bench to confer?"

Permission was granted and Burrows, accompanied by John L. Blevins, one of the prosecuting attorneys, went up to the judge's bench.

I was looking at Wagner while this was taking place, and there was no change in his expression, nor did I see any signs of distress, fear or worry.

He leaned forward a little in his chair to hold a whispered conversation with one of the defense attorneys seated beside him, and smiled sort of wanly as they talked.

Up at the judge's bench, the attorneys were talking in low voices. Both the attorneys and the judge kept poker faces, and I couldn't read anything into their looks, but after a couple of minutes, Judge Chase looked up at the jury. "Do you fix the punishment as death by electrocution or do you fix the punishment as life imprisonment?" he asked.

The spokesman shuffled his feet slightly, keeping his eyes fixed on the judge and away from the prisoner.

"Death by electrocution, your honor," he replied.

Wagner was eyeing the jury closely and paying special attention to the spokesman, that faint smile still hovering around his mouth.

Attorney Burrows asked for as much time as possible in which to make preparations for a motion for a new trial.

"This court will hear your motion for a new trial next Wednesday morning," the judge announced. "Court is adjourned until 9 o'clock Monday morning."

There were about 50 people in the courtroom, and when I got outside, I found that the halls were practically empty. Apparently the anticipated record crowd did not come to hear the outcome of the trial.

And that failure of the crowd to show up had far reaching effects on some.

I left the courthouse right after 8 that morning and drove on over to Bristol to pick up the gear at Bristol Foundry for the feller who had asked me to get it for him.

The workers over at the Bristol Foundry wanted to know the outcome of the trial.

"They found Wagner guilty," I told them, "and they're sending him to the electric chair."

Some of them had figured since it was self-defense, Wagner ought to get off without any punishment, but others said no, he had killed too many, and ought to go to jail over it. None of them seemed to think he ought to be electrocuted over it though, but then they hadn't been on the jury and their opinions didn't count for too much, if you look at it that way.

There had been one little incident that happened just as Wagner was being led from the courtroom that sticks in my mind.

The dentist I mentioned earlier was standing along the wall as the deputies took Wagner past, and he ups and spits on the prisoner!

"You dirty killer!" the dentist said. "You deserve to die. I'm glad they are going to electrocute you!" I was standing fairly close to where they were when it happened. Personally, I couldn't see no call for doing what the dentist done, and if I had been one of the deputies, I believe I'd have smacked him one, but they didn't.

They did stop for just a second, and Wagner's eyes bored into the dentist's with a steady, piercing look that brought a pallor to the toothpuller's face.

"You'll regret that," I thought I heard him say, in a very low, but quiet voice that somehow sent a chill up my own back.

They led Wagner off to a cell and I looked over at the dentist, who was leaning back against the wall, pale and trembling now, as if his effort to tell the prisoner what he thought of him had cost him more than he had bargained for.

And as time went on, it did.

After I loaded the gear up in the trunk of my car, I messed around in Bristol for an hour or so before starting home. So, by the time I got to Blountville, it was close to noon.

The place was nearly deserted. After the huge crowds that had thronged into the little county seat during the past week, it looked like a ghost town. There's something kind of scary about seeing a quick change like that come over a community. I guess I had gotten used to the crowds of people and the busy traffic during that week and now that it was all over, there was sort of a let-down feeling I hadn't expected.

107

It's funny how we get interested in things and go hear or see them, just so we'll be there and know what is happening, never thinking that such events may never happen again, and that our ringside seats in the circus of history can never be repeated.

I had just decided to move on and had reached my hand out to turn my spark and switch to start the car when I heard the sound of an engine just behind me.

I glanced over my shoulder and there was that blamed yellow Buick, nosing its way over the hill. Through the front windscreen, I could see Joe Crum and that out-of-town smarty the car belonged to. They were in the front seat, and it looked like the back seat was all taken up with a big box of some sort.

Joe looked toward me as they roared past, with a grin on his face that stretched nearly from ear to ear. He waved at me in a kind of exaggerated way, sort of like he was showing off and knew it.

After the car passed me, I could see that big box through the back window, and if it held what I figured it held, I knew that ol' Joe's grin was going to turn mighty sour in a very few minutes.

I started up my car and pulled out, driving slowly along behind the yellow car.

Joe and the smart-aleck had gotten out of the car and were looking around at the empty streets in sort of shocked amazement.

"Where is everybody?" Joe asked in a bewildered voice. "We thought there would be a bigger crowd than ever here this morning. Have they moved the trial or something?"

"No," I told him, "it's all over, and they've gone home."

"Oh, my Lord!" he wailed. "We've got 600 hamburgers in the car!"

The out-of-town smarty was in front of Joe in about two jumps.

"You mean to tell me there's nobody here?" he screamed. "Why you ... you ... I ought to beat your brains in!"

Joe's face went from pale to an angry red. "What do you mean, you ought to beat my brains in? This was your idea, buster, and I put in just as much money as you did. You're the wise-guy who said we'd be able to sell more than Potter did if we done it today."

Joe and the out-of-town smarty had thought about my little hamburger selling deal and figured that since people were so interested in the trial that there would be a larger crowd on the last day there to hear the sentencing, and that they'd steal my idea and make a killing selling hamburgers to the hungry crowd.

But what they didn't figure on was that people were interested in the facts, not the outcome and the story, not the ending, so few bothered to come. And besides that, it was Saturday and Saturday is the day most people go to town to do their shopping and such, and they are not about to let something like a historical trial interfere with that. On top of all that, the judge wanted to get it over with as soon as possible, because even a judge has better things to do on a Saturday than to sit in court, so that's what he had done.

Joe and his friend were struck, sure enough..

"What in the world are we going to do with 600 hamburger sandwiches?" Joe wailed.

I finally got the whole story out of them and it was grand, I tell you!

It seems that the out-of-town smarty had got into trouble by parking his car in the judge's reserved space, and had to pay a fine of $50 to get his car out of impound.

To get the $50, he had promised his daddy that he would stay out of trouble and go to work and make the $50 and pay it back.

Then he had pumped Joe, and they schemed and plotted and planned and decided that they would make a killing by selling hamburgers to a hungry crowd on that last day of the trial.

So, they got a feller in Bristol to make them up special, and paid him cash, which took all the money Joe had and left the smart aleck having to borrow $15 on his car to match the $15 Joe put up. They were going to sell the burgers at 15 cents each and make $90, which would give them back their $30 investment and $30 clear profit each, the way they had it figured.

Now, if that wasn't trouble enough, the yellow Buick was blistered with a mortgage on it to the bank and the smart-aleck was paying them $20 a month on it, and he was already behind two payments and the bank had threatened to call his daddy and tell him about it if they didn't get their money right soon.

He still owed $150 on it, he said, and he knew that if his daddy found out what he was doing, he would be forced to pay up or get rid of the car.

Not only that, but he figured he would get packed off to school right quick-like, and he had just started making some headway with the local girls, who thought he was a killer, sure enough.

Well, what could I do?

I bought the hamburgers from them at .02 each for cash, and the car for what was still owed the bank against it, which got Junior off the hook with his daddy and made the bank happy when I paid up the past-due payments.

The hamburgers? I took them in and sold them to Nick for half of whatever he could get out of them. The smart-aleck left town right after that. I drove the yellow Buick a few days and decided I didn't like it after all, it was too flashy and too easy to recognize to be a bachelor's car, and I sold it to Tag Seals, who made another taxi out of it.

Kinnie Wagner got another trial, after his lawyer claimed he hadn't had enough time to prepare properly for the defense, and it was all set to happen again in May. In the meantime, the legends and stories about him grew, if anything, and everybody you talked to seemed to know more about the case than those of us who sat through the trial itself and opinions varied considerably.

For an 8-year old town, Kingsport was sure having an interesting spring!

Kinnie Wagner's Escape
From Sullivan County Jail

During the "roaring" twenties, Kingsport was what you'd have to call a "Boom-Town", I guess. Jay Fred had managed to get George Eastman to buy the government alcohol plant, and the Kodak man had sent in a couple of smart young fellers to run it for him, and they had already built it up, considerable, with a work force that was growing all the time.

Other industries had followed, almost immediately, and within a short span of years, things had changed, sure enough.

By 1925, when Kinnie Wagner had his trouble with the law here, which ended in the shootout on the river bank, business was really humming.

Along the flats, where Center Street was later to be built, the old Grant Leather Tannery had been purchased by some fellers from New York, and they were turning it into a book printing plant, which they had named The Kingsport Press.

An old apple orchard sort of sprawled along between that plant and the town area, and new folks moving to town to try and get jobs at the new industrial plants moved into the orchard area and built temporary tar-paper shacks and tents and all to live in until they got jobs and found houses. It looked like an Indian village, with all the open cookfires and tents and kids running around and yelling and all.

Broad Street had finally got paved, and there were a few buildings scattered along it, with a good many empty lots in between.

Jay Fred had managed to get the town incorporated in 1917, and he put in a "city manager" form of government, which was new to the state and blamed near brand new to the whole country, from what I could tell.

He talked to me some about it one day when I was driving him to Bristol to meet one of his "prospects", a man he hoped to be able to convince that the new town would be an ideal place to put up an automobile factory.

"With the city manager form of government, Pug," he said, "there is no way that a political group can ever get total control of the town and ruin it.

"I donno about that," I told him, right back.

"It seems to me that since you have got a mayor and aldermen that they will have control of the city manager, and run him just the way they want to run him."

"Exactly," he smiled.

I thought about it some and figured out that a city manager system is where you have a mayor and aldermen elected to run the town, but they hire a manager to do it and to take the blame. That way, if things go good, the mayor and aldermen grab the credit and if things go bad, they blame the city manager and fire him.

Under such a system, the mayor and aldermen can promise anything, and everything, to everybody, and blame the city manager for not getting it, if it comes down to that.

At any rate, we had us a mayor, aldermen, and a city manager, and they all done just what Jay Fred told them to do.

Jay Fred had, by the way, sort of broken off from George L. Carter, and had gone to work for John B. Dennis, who was the big New York moneyman in those days and who was in control of The Improvement Company, which owned blamed near everything in sight, except for what the Rollers and a few other folks still had title to, and the mountains all around that Eastman had managed to sew up.

The thing about it was, however, it was working. And you can't hardly argue with success, can you?

But everybody wasn't getting jobs, and not everybody was rich, and things were tough indeed for those folks who were on the outside of the establishment, trying to find a way to get into the inside.

To understand how things were, you have to sort of get over to one side and look back on it from the vantage point of passing time.

The U.S. government had put Prohibition in on January 16, 1920. That didn't just happen overnight, and it wasn't no accident, either. It had been a long time in the making, planning, and a long time in coming.

When Prohibition went into effect, the production of illegal whiskey probably reached an all-time high. It was shipped by case, jug and barrel by railroad to population centers across the land, and fortunes were quickly made for those who controlled its distribution and delivery.

Using special agents, the "hidden middleman" bought up the yield of hundreds of illegal stills scattered through Southwest Virginia and East Tennessee and arranged to transport the moonshine to secret plant locations, where it was strained, flavored, colored and bottled, then delivered to agents of the crime bosses, and eventually found its way to speak easies and private clubs in the larger cities as well as selected smaller towns.

Government agents kept up a running war with the sellers, but never even looked in the direction of the middlemen, who simply sat back and raked in the tremendous profits from their organizational efforts.

Prohibition was one of the greatest boons to the money seekers that had ever been planned out. The best way in the world to build demand for anything is to make it illegal, and, if you are in position to supply that demand, you can just about name your own price, and for 13 years, from 1920 until 1933, the money poured in at an unbelievable rate.

During these years, the developing city of Kingsport enjoyed an unprecedented growth, unlike any other city in the country, and enjoyed a prosperity heretofore unknown in the mountains of East Tennessee.

The stock market crash of October, 1929, marked the beginning of the end of those days of fast profits and easy cash, for a panicked nation began to worry about its rights and privileges along with many other problems, and pressure would be brought on legislators to repeal the Prohibition laws, considered by some to be a violation of American freedom of choice.

It was only after the repeal of Prohibition that the Depression's grim effects began to be felt in the modern little town on the banks of the Holston River, at least in any major sort of way.

When Kinnie Wagner's first trial for the murder of Kingsport policeman John Smith ended at Blountville in the young circus performers conviction and death sentence, the attorneys for the defense immediately entered a motion for a new trial. Judge Guy S. Chase ruled that he would hear the motion and arguments on it the following Monday, and this created a lot of interest and talk around Kingsport.

A bunch of us men were setting around in Shaffers Restaurant drinking Cokes or coffee and talking about it, and the case pretty well got itself tried all over again right there at the table.

"Why, they ain't a blamed bit of use in trying him again," Slip Sampson said.

"They know he is guilty. He even SAID he shot them fellers. The way I see it, there ain't no two ways about it, he just up and killed

113

them and that's final. So they were right in convicting him, it seems to me."

"Yeah, Slip, but that don't go far enough. He shot them, alright, no argument about that, but the thing is, if they shot at him FIRST, didn't he do just what anybody else would do, or ought to?" Clem Culbertson put in.

"But, blame it, THEY all claim HE shot first," Slip insisted.

"Well, if you wus a policeman, and you went out to shoot a feller down, and he up and shot you instead, wouldn't YOU claim that too, no matter what REALLY happened?" Clem was beginning to rock Slip's firm conviction.

"What if THEY DID actually go down there trying to kill him just to get that reward. What if they DID go running up there, guns already drawn and blazing away? If you had of been Kinnie, and it happened to you, and you had a gun and was a mighty fine shot on your own, what would YOU do?"

"Well," Slip said slowly, thinking hard about it, "if it was like THAT, I reckon I'd jump behind a tree or something and shoot right back at them, if they just come running up a shooting at me."

"Ain't that right, Pug? You was up there at the trial, wasn't you? Ain't that what HE said?"

I hadn't meant to get into the argument over it all, because I was kind of tired of it by this time, but I had been to the trial, and all of the men around the table knew it.

"That's about it", I told them. "Kinnie Wagner said at the trial that he shot at them AFTER they shot at him. He said he figured they knew about the $1,000 reward for him, dead or alive, and they meant to collect it by killing him right on the spot. So he shot them first."

"There!" Clem beamed with satisfaction, having proven his point to his own satisfaction.

"That's why they have to give him a new trial, don'tcha see?"

But Slip wasn't ready to give up yet.

"No, blame it, I don't see. The jury convicted him even after HEARING all that. Just because HE said one thing and the OFFICERS said another thing, that ain't the point. The point is, who did the JURY believe, the officers, on account of they found Wagner guilty. So why give him a new trial? That's just a waste of the taxpayers' money."

"It's on account of there is more to it all than we have heard so far," Clem said.

"You just wait, you'll find out, when the new trial comes up."

"You see," he leaned over closer across the table and dropped his voice to a hoarse whisper, "I KNOW about two fellers who SAW IT ALL. And they are going to swear that the police started shooting FIRST!"

I could tell right then that the Kinnie Wagner story was not nearly over yet. Which it wasn't.

For once, Clem Culbertson turned out to be right. When the Criminal Court convened the next day at Blountville, Judge Guy S. Chase announced that he had decided to grant Kinnie Wagner a new trial.

I wasn't there at the time, but I could imagine the defense attorneys trying to keep from looking too pleased, in order to retain their courtroom decorum.

Defense lawyers Burrows, Warren and Cox were all present, I found out later, to hear the announcement.

They had carefully prepared their motion, and it contained sixteen major points, all claiming that Wagner had been unjustly convicted.

The main key to the motion, it was said, was that the defense attorneys had found three new witnesses who had SEEN the shooting, and that all of them were willing to swear that the officers drew first and started shooting at Wagner before he ever shot back!

The witnesses were named in the newspaper that day. They were Robert Bowman, of Johnson City, and Nathan Langford, Sr., and Nathan Langford, Jr., both of Kingsport.

I didn't know the Langfords myself, but it wasn't long before I run into somebody who said they knew them, knew them well, and had known them all their lives, and knew they wouldn't lie.

That kind of put a kink in the rope of conviction the lawyers and the law had pulled so tightly around the young circus performer, at least to my mind. If the police DID go down there with drawn guns, blasting away at Wagner and trying to kill him, that meant they were really after the cash reward of $1,000 just like he had said all along, and they maybe got about what they deserved.

At least a lot of people in Kingsport started thinking so when they found out about the affidavits the Langford men had signed.

It is kind of a matter of conscience with most folks. They believe in the law, but they have seen too much out of law officers to trust them whole-heartedly, and usually with good reason. So as long as the facts back up what officers claim, folks tend to get outraged at criminals who break the law or shoot at one of the lawmen, especially if they hit him.

But when one of their own kind, a private citizen who has no ax to grind nor any paycheck to protect, comes up and says he saw it all, the officers are telling lies about it, that confidence in the law is badly shaken.

If that witness is backed up by two more witnesses who tell it the same way, why, you can pretty well bet that most people will take THEIR word over the law's anytime, and again with good reason.

Just because a man has a badge pinned on his shirt does not mean that he is more likely to tell the truth than anybody else may be.

If these new witnesses were truthful, then it became the general feeling that young Kinnie Wagner had suffered great wrong at the hands of the law, and that his actions in shooting back were justified and reasonable.

All that weekend, the controversy over whether Kinnie Wagner had been treated fairly kept growing. The law-and-order fellers, which included most of the lawyers and the newspaper, as well as the deputies and officers, kept insisting that he had already been found guilty and that a second trial was just a waste of the taxpayers' money.

I've noticed that when fellers like that start talking about is "wasting the taxpayers' money" they are angling around to get something fixed up in the best interest of all concerned or not. At other times, when they are on the other side, they talk about the "required investment in improvement", and they are talking about the same blamed thing, but just on a different side of it!

It began to be a sort of contest of those in power and the rest of the people. If Kinnie Wagner had shot first, the law was probably right. But, if like these new witnesses said they were willing to swear, the officers had started shooting first, that put a whole different blush on the rose, if you understand what I mean. Most people on the street seemed to understand it that way.

When it gets to the place that the law goes around shooting first and asking questions later, we are in hot water, sure enough.

Clifford Bates and Hump Ferguson come in to Shaffer's Restaurant while I was eating a hamburger, and they sat down beside me and started talking about it.

"Why," Hump said, "if them officers went down there and just started out shooting, like them witnesses said, they could have killed some of them girls that were there."

"Well, they probably wouldn't have hit none of the girls, on account of Wagner run off down the river away from where they were at", Clifford put in, "but they sure must have been trying to kill Wagner, if that's what they done.

"That's just plain old murder," Hump said. "I don't see how they can be allowed to get away with that."

"What somebody ought to do", Clifford lowered his voice a bit and leaned forward across the table, "is to just go up there to Blountville and help bust Wagner out of jail."

He leaned back away from the table and glanced around the room to see if anybody was listening. "They are not going to let him have a fair trial, if they DID try to kill him. They can't afford to let it be known, so they will have to convict him. And the lawyers and all are on their side, because if the OFFICERS turn out looking like crooks, THEY will, too."

"You reckon Wagner'd leave the country if somebody DID help him get out?" Hump was obviously intrigued with the thought.

"Why, sure he would. He was starting to leave when the shooting mess happened. He didn't have no mind to stay around these parts no way. And who can blame him?"

Well, the talk went on that way for some time, and finally Hump and Clifford decided to go someplace else, and they left.

I got up and paid my bill and started out the door, and then I just happened to glance back around the restaurant dining room and I saw Deputy Sheriff Joe Thomas peeking his head up over the high booth he had been hiding in, listening to every word that had been said!

It dawned on me real quick that if Wagner DID happen to bust out of jail, with or without help, in the next few days, I would be in trouble as a suspect, right along with Hump and Clifford.

When you are in a spot like that, the best thing to do is handle it right away. So I put on a big smile and hollered out: "Hey, Joe, did you hear all that nonsense the boys were joking about? Funny, wasn't it?"

Sheriff Thomas' face got kind of red, and he nodded, trying to force an answering smile onto his face. But he couldn't quite succeed.

When Jay Fred called me the next morning, at my boarding house, I knew something important must be up.

"Pug," he said, "can you drive over to Bristol for me this morning?"

If he had planned on going, he would have asked if I could take him to Bristol, so I knew he wanted to send me to pick up something, or maybe somebody.

"Wait while I check my calendar," I told him. I didn't have a blamed thing to do that day that couldn't wait, but I had heard him use that same line on fellers several times, and figured it was due to come back at him.

After pausing a minute, I told him I could manage to squeeze such a trip in, by re-arranging a couple of things and delaying some others.

"Good!" he said. "Go to the Majestic movie house at 11:00 a.m. and pick up a Mr. Holt. He's coming to Kingsport to see about remodeling the Gem Theatre, as the representative of the owners. I'll call him and let him know that you'll be there."

I got to Bristol a little early, and messed around the town for a while, waiting until time to pick up Mr. Holt. The messing around resulted in a date with a good-looking girl with reddish-brown hair and green eyes for the following Saturday night, which is what makes messing around worthwhile.

Mr. Holt was ready and waiting promptly at 11:00 a.m., just like he was supposed to be. He had a couple of suit cases sitting on the curb, too, indicating that he planned to stay a while when he finally got to where he was going.

He was a fattish man, about forty, with a red face and a friendly smile and firm handshake.

"I appreciate you being here right on time," he said. "Mr. Johnson said you were dependable. I've had a lot of work to do over here and will have a whole lot more in Kingsport. I'm going to stay over there for several weeks, I think."

When he finally paused for breath, I got his suitcases loaded up in the back seat and he climbed into the front with me, and we started rolling back toward Kingsport.

It was hot in the car, but I had opened the windows and pushed the window-wings out as far as I could.

I had rigged up my windshield with a bug screen earlier that spring, after a bad experience with a bumblebee.

That had happened on a pleasant (otherwise) Sunday afternoon, coming back from a picnic up at the reservoir with Mildred Tibbs.

Mildred is a kind of high-strung girl anyway, you might say, and when the big bumblebee got in the car through the open front windshield and sort of landed in her hair, she kind of what you might call cut a fit.

The blamed bee didn't even sting her. It stung me instead, when I was trying to get her out of the car to make sure she wasn't hurt or anything.

We had words over it before I got her home, and I haven't been back since.

But I did rig up a bug screen to make sure I wouldn't have to go through nothing like that again, no matter who I was with, high-strung or not.

Before you could know it, we were rolling right in to Blountville, Sullivan County's sleepy little county seat.

Suddenly, Holt grabbed my arm. He was gazing out the window toward the upstairs bars of the jail. "Look there!" he exclaimed. "Those men are trying to break the bars loose!"

I slammed on the brakes and jerked the car to a stop in the middle of the road, peering past Holt through the open car window on his side.

I could just barely see the upper part of the jail building around behind the courthouse. At an upstairs barred window, toward the middle of the building, I could see movement taking place.

If Holt hadn't of been looking right in that direction during the split second he saw a flash of movement, the chances are a thousand to one that we would have never known about what was taking place. But, as we sat there in the hot car and watched, an object of some sort slammed into the barred window from inside, smashing some of the glass from the pane and hammering against the outside bars.

Behind the object, which looked like a big wide frame of some sort, we could see men's faces, visible in the late morning sunshine that poured against the windows of the jail.

'They're trying to break out!" Holt exclaimed, and I had to agree with him.

"Quick," I told him, "let's get down there and tell the jailer!"

The men at the window saw us coming on the run, but they didn't slow down any, as far as I could tell, and just kept on slamming the thing they were using against the window bars.

We raced down the hill and around the building to the door, and Holt burst through it, me right on his heels.

A woman was standing in the little office just off the entry way. She looked up with a start as we came slamming in.

"Quick!" Holt yelled at her. "Call the jailer! There are some men upstairs trying to break out!"

"He's already up there!" the woman replied. "We just found out about it, and he's gone up to stop them."

She seemed nervous, but not too worried about it. We found out that she was Mrs. Barr, the jailers wife, and that she and her husband lived in the house back there beside of the jail.

After a few minutes, the jailer, Barr, came back downstairs, having got things under control up there in the lockup, and got the prisoners all back in cells where they were supposed to be.

He told us what had happened, and how the prisoners had nearly managed a breakout.

Barr and his wife were over at their house, getting ready to eat lunch. But Barr kept smelling something burning, and recalled that the odor had been even stronger as he walked around the back of the jail a few minutes earlier.

Thinking that something might be on fire up there, with a good many confined prisoners who would be defenseless and at the mercy of a fire, Barr decided to go investigate.

He must have been going up the stairs just about the time Holt had seen the men slamming something against the barred windows of the jail.

The burning smell was from blankets the prisoners had set on fire deliberately, for the dangest reason you could think about …one that had almost worked, too!

What the prisoners had done, Barr, the jailer, said, was pull the chains loose from a couple of cots in the cell.

"They knew what they were doing, alright", he said.

"A few more minutes, and they'd have been out that window!"

Barr said he reckoned that ONE of the prisoners, although he did not say WHICH one, must have known all about breaking out of a jail cell.

"What they did was," he explained, "they got them chains loose from the cots and took the blankets and piled 26 them under the cell door and set them on fire."

He rolled his eyes a little when he talked, showing that he was still sort of excited about it all.

"They put them chains through the bars of the cell door and yanked on it when the metal got hot from the blanket fire, and got it right off of its hinges!"

It had been the cell door we had seen them hammering against the window bars.

Barr said they had managed to bend the window bars pretty good, and had one bar loose at one end by the time he caught them.

There were some fifteen of the prisoners involved in the jailbreak attempt, but when Barr walked in on them with a big pistol already in his hand, cocked and ready to blast away, they laid down the cell door and raised their hands in surrender.

"That's the first trouble we've had since HE'S been back," Barr said, and I knew right away he meant Kinnie Wagner!

It had slipped my mind that Wagner was back in the Blountville jail, having been returned from Knoxville just a few days earlier for the date to be set on the new trial he had been given.

There had been gossip and talk about the possibility that the now famous gunman might try to escape jail, but I hadn't paid much attention to it, because you always hear that kind of stuff, and not much of it ever actually happens.

"The blamed county is so tight, it won't keep guards up here during the day," Barr said, "and I got to look after all of it by myself. They have two full-time armed guards at night, all the time, because they figure that if HE tried to break out, it will be some time after dark, for some reason."

"But he is just as likely to try to bust out during the day, and I've been trying to tell them that. I can't be up there every minute of the time during the day, I've got too much to do. I'm going to try and get them to put a couple of guards on during the daytime, too, at least until the trial comes up and is over with." Barr said that the newspaper accounts of how cheerful and friendly Wagner was were sort of slanted, in his opinion.

"When they first brought him up here, he was quiet enough", the jailer said, "but every day that goes by finds him a little more on edge."

He rubbed a hand over the back of his head and it came away wet with sweat.

"That is one edgy prisoner, I tell you," he declared.

He said that Wagner had, of late, begun to throw food and things at his captors and even other prisoners, and had got short-tempered and ready to cuss anybody out who didn't look at him just right.   The other prisoners were wary of him, Barr said, and tried to stay out of his way, except for one or two who felt important by associating with Wagner as much as they could.

But they all were in awe of the powerful and deadly youth, the jailer said.

"I tell you, men, if he ordered them to help him, they wouldn't refuse," he said.

"And that ain't because they'd WANT to do it, mind you, but on account of they'd be AFRAID to not do what he asked." He shook his head and breathed a deep sigh.

"And the way that boy can GLARE! I tell you, boys, I'm half afraid of him myself, even when I know I've got a gun and he ain't got one. He looks like he could just about shoot you with his eyes, he can look so mad and mean!"

When the word got out that Kinnie Wagner had been involved in an attempted jail break, it caused a flurry of excitement.

Folks had been speculating about just that sort of thing happening, anyway, and nobody seemed very much surprised. They said they had been expecting it all along.

The sheriff went before the County Court and asked for extra funds which would allow him to put on daytime guards at the jail, in addition to the night time guards who were already on duty.

After hemming and hawing around a while, like County Court always does, they approved the money, like they always do, so two extra guards were hired to work the day shift.

What puzzled me over it was that Kinnie Wagner was just one of the sixteen prisoners who attempted the breakout, but he is the one who got mentioned most, and the one who got credit for the whole scheme and plan.

I had checked around a little, with some deputies I happen to know, and found out that there were several among the sixteen who were rough and ready, dangerous men. And, from what I heard, two or three of them might well be far worse than the Wagner boy ever thought about being, and had very likely done some killing of their own, but not in a stand-up shootout fight where the other fellows could shoot back. Rather, the kind of crimes they were suspected of lay more in the ambush-from-hiding sort of thing.

Wagner had, as far as I could find out, stood up and shot it out with the officers who went after him down there by the river, and, from all the testimony I had heard, it seemed very possible that his self-defense argument was well worth considering.

Down at Rollers Store, in Old Kingsport, the next morning, a milk truck driver was busy switching cases of milk and cream from one truck to another. He had started out early that day, but the truck he was driving developed a bad knock in the motor, so he called his employer, Altmont Dairy, which was located not far away, and had someone bring another truck down to Roller's.

John Hickman, the milk truck driver, started unloading cases of milk and cream from his sick truck and putting them on the one that had been brought down for him. He had parked his truck, the one with the knock in the engine, in front of Roller's, and the replacement truck was parked on the opposite side of the road, so Hickman was taking cases off of the bad-engine truck and toting them across the road to the other vehicle.

After making a half dozen trips with just two or three cases stacked up on top of each other, Hickman decided to try a lazy-man's load, and stacked up as many cases as he could lift at one time, six of them, towering up higher than his head, and kind of wobbling a little as he carried them across the road.

It was on the fourth heavily-loaded trip across the road that the car came barrelling along down Sullivan Street and didn't see Hickman.

Needless to say, Hickman didn't see the car either, nor even hear it, because there was so much noise from the running truck motor and other sounds about the store.

The milkman was right in the middle of the road, the tall stack of cream cases reaching high over his head, when the driver of the car looked up and saw him, far too late to stop, although he slammed on his brakes as hard as possible.

The car smacked into Hickman, sending bottles of cream shooting off through the air in several directions, and knocking the unfortunate milkman up in the air only to fall down right on the hot hood of the vehicle and roll forward to the front bumper, while the car skidded along the roadway, trying to get stopped. Hickman actually got pulled under the front of the car, and rolled off on the pavement, while the car passed right over him.

As the car finally rolled to a stop, Hickman lay in a flat heap behind it, and sat up, rubbing his head and looking around for his scattered bottles of cream!

He was taken down to the Riverview Hospital, to be checked over and treated for injuries about his head and shoulders, but they said he would recover alright.

I had gone down to Shaffer's Restaurant on Broad Street to eat that Friday evening, and was just biting into my second big hamburger when this newspaper boy came busting in through the door, hollering "EXTRA!" and waving a handful of newspapers around.

I could see the headlines all across the front page, in close to what they call "Second Coming type". It must have been at least four or five inches tall, bold and black:

"K. WAGNER BREAKS JAIL," it said.

I tossed the boy a nickel and got a copy to read while I ate my hamburger.

Smaller headlines ran across the page under the big one, just like some of the big city newspapers set them.

"Desperate Gunman and 6 Companions Overpower Jailer Barr".

I skimmed through them and read down to the story.

"Kinnie Wagner and 6 other prisoners overpowered the jailer and two guards at the county jail at Blountville, and made their escape shortly before 6 o'clock this afternoon.

"All 7 of the men are still at large, and it is known that at least 3 of them, including Wagner, are armed with guns, taken from the jailer and guards.

"The men escaping were Kinnie Wagner, Bart Davenport, of Kingsport, Don Taylor, Andy Wilson, Charles Grose, Ed Cutsinger and Harry Williamson. They made their escape after the two guards had brought in the crew of prisoners who had been working on the road. The guards, with Jailer Barr had gone upstairs to the prisoners' cage and Jailer Barr had opened the door to admit two other prisoners when Wagner and the other 6 men rushed out.

"One of the prisoners hit the jailer over the head with a Coca-Cola bottle, and Wagner and the others pounced upon him and the other guards and took their guns. A .38 Special was taken from Barr and .38 Automatics were taken from each of the guards. It is known that Wagner has one of the .38's and Davenport has another. One member of the escaping party also has a shotgun.

"After overpowering the jailer and the guards the prisoners rushed down the stairway and out the first opening which came to their convenience. Two of the men made their exit at the rear door and another through the kitchen windows.

124

"Davenport was the first to come out the front door, according to R. C. Carter, a helper at the jail, who was outside at the time the prisoners escaped.

"Carter stated that he could have shot Davenport just after he came out the front door, had a woman not stepped in behind him, between him and the prisoner. He stated he had his gun pointed at Davenport when Wagner stepped out the front door and fired at him, but missed.

"After this, he said Davenport and Wagner ran out the Reedy Creek Road about 100 feet and left the road, going across the road into a woodland, known as Brown's Woodland.

"It is reported that a man shot Wagner while he was going out the road and that he fell to the ground, quickly picking himself up, and continued across the field. This report, however, has not been fully authenticated.

"The other 5 prisoners were seen to go along the creek which comes into Blountville from the north.

"Posses were organized amid the frantic spell which hit the county seat and more deputies and citizens were joining in the search each hour with the hopes of apprehending the fugitives before nightfall.

"Citizens of Blountville were deputized and joined in the search armed with almost every weapon imaginable. Police headquarters have been notified at Bristol, Kingsport, Gate City, Johnson City and other cities, and the entire country is being combed in the frantic search for the prisoners.

"A scene of turmoil and confusion prevailed at Blountville this afternoon when the prisoners made their getaway.

"A number of other prisoners in the jail could have escaped had they been so inclined.

"Cries of the women inmates in the jail could be heard over the entire village amid the scrambling of feet and the marshalling of force.

"Sheriff Joe Thomas arrived at Blountville shortly after the prisoners made their escape and has taken up the pursuit with the posse.

"A network is being laid through which it is seemingly impossible for the fugitives to elude their captors."

As the story that Kinnie Wagner had escaped from Blountville jail got around, it stirred up about as much excitement as the shooting down on the river had generated.

People were out running up and down the streets, asking everyone they met if they had heard about it, in hopes of being the bearer of exciting news, and thereby sharing in a bit of reflected glory.

The law in Kingsport didn't waste much time, either. They got a crowd together and formed a posse, just like the sheriff had done up in Blountville, in case Wagner had decided to come our way.

It is my personal suspicion that they would have vastly preferred that he not do so, and the busy searches they conducted all seemed to be in well-lighted places. Some of the folks up Blountville way might have been foolhardy enough to go after Wagner in the dark, but the people of Kingsport had learned first hand of his shooting skills, and had no desire to see them once again demonstrated.

Although it sounded from the news reports at the time as if the Blountville posse was diligently searching for Wagner and the other escapees, the story I got later was that they deliberately searched in a direction that was opposite of the way he had been seen taking, a prudent move, you might say, for safety's sake.

Dr. Will Hutchins left immediately for Florida. He did not bother to inform his dental patients that he would be away from his office for an indefinite period of time, but called his office girl from Knoxville and instructed her to put a card on his door saying the office was closed.

According to talk around town, the dentist had been present at the Kingsport Police station when Wagner was first brought in on his way to the Blountville jail, after his surrender to a private citzen over near Waycross, Virginia.

They say the tooth-yanker spat on Wagner as he was led down the hall in handcuffs and armchains. I don't know if it is true or not, but the story is all over town, and, they say, Wagner looked him right in the eye and told him that he would "get him for that" someday.

At any rate, the dentist took off on his sudden unannounced trip to Florida fast enough to lend credibility to the tale.

Folks claimed later that when the attempted jailbreak had taken place the week before, that Hutchins left so quickly and traveled so fast he was past Chattanooga and headed toward Atlanta before word caught up to him that it was a false alarm.

In Kingsport, the law kept searching the best-lighted streets and avoiding dark alleys and other such places.

I don't know as I blamed them, for I had a bit of trouble walking into dark streets myself for the next few nights.

126

Wagner was reported seen all over town, as well as in Bristol, Johnson City, Norton, Gate City and even Rogersville. If any one man could have traveled as much and gone as far and as fast as the rumors held that the desperado had done, there would never be any chance of capturing him again, I figured.

Over in Bristol, the law surrounded the home of Ed Cutsinger, one of the escapees who broke out with Wagner, and threatened to start shooting right through the walls until everybody inside came out with their hands up.

Cutsinger's family came out, children and all, with hands held high, but the escaped prisoner was not among them. He had already been there and was long gone, a good hour before the law even showed up. I figured it was considerate of them to give him ample time for a visit before they came roaring in, ready to shoot on sight anything that moved.

It didn't look to me like it would be very hard to figure out which way Wagner went after he and the others broke out of Blountville jail.

He was born and raised over in Scott County, Virginia, which was a pretty well-known fact, and had a lot of relatives over that way.

All he had to do after he left the jail was take a right turn and head for the state line, which is only five or six miles due north.

Of course, he could have got foxy and gone the other way, figuring that the law would figure that he had gone the way I figured he would go, so he would go the other way to out-figure them. In that case, all he had to do was head due south, veering a little to the south, and he could reach the Holston River's South Fork, where he could grab a floating log and drift all the way to Rotherwood, below Kingsport, where another right turn would put him on the North Fork of the river and take him right back to the county of his birth, safely across the state line.

There would have been very little sense in his going toward Bristol or Kingsport, but the law searched in those towns just like they expected to find him standing under a street lamp, waiting for them to come along and pick him up.

There was even talk that he might head for North Carolina, but that didn't make much sense to me.

The officers searched carefully all around Blountville Courthouse and through that neighborhood, but I noticed that they gave Wagner plenty of time to get a good way from there before they began the search.

127

Knowing that he had a .38 pistol and was a dead shot could have had a little something to do with that.

The newspaper accounts of the escape got twisted a little more each day, until there was so many heroes shooting at Wagner and the others as they made out, you couldn't hardly understand how none of them managed to get hit.

From the first reports I had, there wasn't a shot fired in the entire escape. But after a few hours passed, different folks got to admitting how they had almost shot Wagner, but just narrowly missed him each time, even though they emptied their guns at him all the way from a distance to point-blank range.

One of the guards said he had a shootout with Davenport, who came out the jail door just in front of Wagner, and that Wagner then came running out shooting at him while Davenport grabbed a woman and held her in front of the pair of them as a shield. The jailers wife admitted that she emptied a whole pistol at Wagner without hitting him a single time, and even a trustee at the jail, Walter Dunn, claimed he grabbed a rifle and took several pot-shots at the ring-leader of the break as he and Davenport made off down the road toward the woods.

Folks believed about anything they read or heard about it, too. But I couldn't hardly figure out how a trustee, who is a prisoner himself, could get a hold of a rifle if the jail had been running as smoothly as it ought to have been, and it seemed kind of strange to me that the jailers wife would just happen to be standing around with a pistol in her hand when it all took place.

By the following Sunday, the manhunt was still on, but growing a little more useless every hour. Several people I knew joined in one or another of the posses that were being formed, and took a turn at looking over the countryside, mostly in places I don't think Wagner would have gone to even if the law was right behind him.

But the newspaper played up the story about as big as a declaration of war.

"MANHUNT IS YET OF NO AVAIL," the headline screamed. "Wagner and Companions Are Still At Large As Officers Continue Searching County, Believe Desperado Is in Familiar Country."

Well, blame it, of COURSE he was in familiar country. He was RAISED around here, and HAD to be familiar with it!

And everybody already knew that the manhunt was "of no avail", providing they knowed what that word "avail" meant.

Slip Simpson got confused over it.

"What do they need a avail fer?" he asked me. "They gonna try to HAMMER some irons or chains onto him when they catch him?"

I had to explain to him that what he was thinking about was an ANVIL, which was a whole different thing than "avail".

I read through the newspaper story, but there wasn't a whole lot new in it.

"Kinnie Wagner, instinctive slayer and desperado, has been successful in eluding his pursuers since he and 6 other prisoners executed a dramatic jail delivery at Blountville late Friday afternoon", it said.

You could tell that by using the word "delivery" to mean escape, the writer was getting all set to pound out a story that was nothing new at all, but would just rehash all the known facts to date. When newspaper writers start using words that are alright, but don't quite fit, so the reader has to stop and think about it for a minute or two to figure out just what they mean, you can bet it is going to be that kind of story. Why do you reckon they do that? Everybody knows what they are trying to do, and it would make a heap more sense to just tell it in plain language and go on to something else that WAS news. But they'll do it every time.

"While hundreds of officers and citizens of Sullivan, Washington and Scott Counties have been combing the country for the fugitives, no trace has been found of the desperate character who so cleverly schemed the getaway Friday.

"It has been reported that Wagner has been seen in Virginia and near the North Carolina line at different times, but none of these reports have been sufficiently authenticated and consequently no one knows where the slayer is hiding.

"A deputy sheriff phoned into Blountville yesterday and stated that he had seen Wagner cross the Reedy Creek Road near Ford's Store. Officers rushed to the scene but it is not known what results were accomplished."

All of that could have been summed up in a short sentence or two, but newspaper writers like to get wordy when they can, especially when they don't have anything to say.

They are sort of like Finnigan, who was a line crew boss on the Clinchfield Railroad in the early days.

The superintendent's name was Flannigan, and Finnigan had to write reports to Flannigan every time a car got off the tracks and had to be put back on.

Flannigan was a stickler for written reports and insisted on them, but Finnigan was not a person who had an outstanding aptitude for using words.

Yet, he tried. And his laborious, detailed, handwritten epistles got to be just too much for Superintendent Flannigan to bear.

So Flannigan wrote to Finnigan and told him that, in all future reports, which were to be made on time and promptly, he, Finnigan, was to give all details but give them briefly.

It hurt Finnigan's feelings, it did. So the next time a car got off the tracks, Finnigan took his crew and got it back on, and sent in his report immediately.

"Superintendent Flannigan:

"Off again. On again. Gone again. Finnigan."

Sometimes I think it would be better if Finnigan wrote the newspaper stories and the fellow who writes the newspaper spent his time putting cars back on the railroad tracks.

I turned back to the newspaper story and waded through the rest of it.

"Erroneous Reports," the sub-head read.

"Reports were circulated early yesterday morning that Wagner held up two men on the Bloomingdale Road late Friday night and took some money from them. W.H. Newland, one of the men reported to have been held up, denied any knowledge of the affair in a communication with the newspaper yesterday morning.

"It was also reported that when Wagner was seen near the North Carolina line, he relieved a person of a sum of money and warned him not to let it be known that he had been seen.

"Officers yesterday surrounded the residence of Abe Cutsinger, member of the escaping party who lives in Bristol, but the prisoner had been home and left an hour or so before the officers arrived.

"While the 3 men were disarming Barr, others in the escaping party were wrestling with Guard Blackburn," the news story said.

"After knocking him down and relieving him of his pistol the men rushed down the stairs and met Deputy Weaver at the foot."

It seemed to me if I had been a deputy and was down at the foot of the stairs going up to the jail, and heard 3 men come galloping down the steps, I would have pulled out my pistol and been standing there waiting on them, gun already drawn. But that was not what happened.

"They immediately covered the deputy with one of the pistols procured from above and relieved him of his weapon. A shotgun was also procured on the way out of the building.

"Wagner and Davenport were the first to leave the building. They made their exit through the side door of the jail, next to the jailer's residence.

"Davenport came first, according to a statement of R. C. Carter, guard, who was standing outside at the time of the escape.

"Carter said that Davenport opened fire upon him when he came out. Carter returned the fire and said he could have shot Davenport had he not held Hazel Dunn in front of him.

"Wagner soon appeared and also fired at Carter but none of the bullets took effect.

"It is presumed that Wagner fired at the guard only to keep him back rather than with intentions to kill, since he is so crafty with a pistol.

"On Reedy Creek Road - Following their exits from the jail, Wagner and Davenport took the Reedy Creek Road from about 100 yards away from the jail. In the course of their escape some shots were fired at Wagner while in pursuit of him out the road.

"Mrs. Barr, the jailer's wife, emptied a revolver at the fugitives.

"Wagner was seen to leave the road and crawl under a fence and disappear into the woods.

"Dunn claims he saw Wagner fall after one of his shots, but it is not probable that either of the bullets took effect. "The prisoners were not in any hurry to getaway, Carter said. They walked out of the jail, he stated. Wagner, with pistol in hand, appeared the same self-confident, instinctive killer...with his characteristic poise restored, not afraid to stand and shoot it out if the occasion demanded.

"Wagner is alleged to have killed a deputy sheriff in Mississippi on last Christmas Day and he was in hiding here when he committed the double murder on the banks of the Holston River on April 13.

"A reward of $1,000 had been offered for his return to Mississippi by authorities, dead or alive.

"The officers killed here were Policeman John Smith and Deputy Sheriff H. D. Webb. Policeman George Frazier was seriously wounded at the time the other officers were slain. Wagner made a hasty getaway after the gun battle here, but gave himself up to a citizen at Waycross, Virginia, the following morning and was taken to Blountville jail. A few weeks later he was tried in the Sullivan County

Court.   The jury in the case found the accused guilty and recommended punishment by death in the electric chair. A new trial was granted on the technical errors presented by the defense and was set for June 22.   At this time, the state made a motion for a continuance of the trial on the grounds that 3 of its witnesses were absent, the trial was continued until August 17.

I went back up the column and read over it again just to make sure it said what I understood it to say.   From this news story, it was evident that the law and the newspaper, which was inclined to write what it was told rather than what it found out for itself, had decided that Wagner was totally guilty, regardless of what the outcome of a new trial might have been.

All those colorful adjectives like "instinctive slayer" and "double murderer" made that obvious.

But if all the people who claimed they had been shooting at Wagner as he walked down the road toward the woods missed as easy as that, it sort of looked to me like that if they ever caught him, what they ought to do is get him to give the guards and such a few lessons in what to do with guns if the time permits before they get around to electrocuting him.

There was more, even if it didn't tell much.

But one of the escaping prisoners HAD been picked up just a few hours after the breakout and getaway, so that gave the newspaper something to pad the story out some more with.

"Don Taylor, caught late Friday, is the only one of the seven prisoners escaping that has been apprehended. Officers are believing that Wagner has singled out himself and is hiding in a place selected before the escape.

"Others believe he is hiding close around Blountville. Some believe he is near here and yet the majority of people believe he is several miles out of this section.

"Posses are yet searching and bending every energy in an effort at apprehending the notorious desperado and the other prisoners.

"Several members of the posse have returned to their homes, worn out by an all day and night search, while others have taken up the search in their place.

"County Wide Search.....

"Hundreds of officers and citizens combed the country Friday night, bending every energy possible to recapture the super criminal and his 5 companions.

"Don Taylor, a member of the escaping party was captured shortly after the escape and was placed behind the iron bars again.

"He had very little to say about the sensational escape, but did not deny that he threw the combination to Wagner's cell which let the desperado free. He stated that he had not planned to escape with the other prisoners and that it came so sudden he didn't know much about it.

"Wagner acted as ring leader in the dramatic delivery and exercised good judgment in choosing his time for the escape. He no doubt realized that Jailer Barr saw him safely behind the bars in his own cell and that he would feel no fear of the others.

"The suddenness with which the delivery was started and the prompt action of the prisoners contributed largely to the scheme.

"Carefully Planned….."

"While the road prisoners were out at work Friday, the other prisoners and Wagner carefully planned their escape. Two or three of the prisoners had managed to free themselves from the cage in which they were confined and had concealed themselves in the small hall leading from the stairway.

"When Jailer Barr, with Guard McCoy Blackburn and Deputy Sheriff John Weaver approached the cage entrance to admit the road prisoners, the men concealed in the corridor hurled themselves at the jailer while Taylor threw the combination to free Wagner and the others.

"Jailer Barr came near to frustrating the clever scheme when he put up a spirited battle in the corridor of the hall, but he was against heavy odds and after his gun was taken and thrust against his breast, he was helpless.

"Wagner had instructed his companions in planning the delivery and each man knew just what he should do. He had, no doubt, impressed the importance of securing as many weapons as possible, since the prisoners took all they could find.

"Bert Davenport struck the jailer over the head with some sort of blackjack and knocked him in the corner.

"When Cutsinger and Wilson came to Davenport's aid, we three went to the floor", Jailer Barr said.

"They then took his pistol, keys and some ammunition and locked him in a cell."

I read that over a second time, trying to figure it out.

If the jailer had been blackjacked and knocked into a corner, how could he have been struggling with the three prisoners at the same time?

Right after that, talk got out about how many attempts had been made to smuggle guns or other weapons to Wagner while he had been held prisoner in the Blountville jail.

The newspaper carried news stories about it, claiming it was so. But it seemed strange that they hadn't reported any of that sort of thing when it happened, if it did.

"Several attempts have been made to smuggle arms into the prisoner's cell at Blountville," one such story run, "by which it was intended for him to make an escape.

"Wagner came near breaking jail last week after a door had been torn from its hinges and several of the prisoners were out of their cells. The attempt was frustrated by Jailer Barr.

"County authorities regard Wagner as one of the most disagreeable characters ever held in the Blountville jail.

"He has been a menace to the guards and other prisoners of the jail and has boasted that he would not stay there very long."

Well, if it was true that he had been boasting that he wouldn't stay long, it was true, because they couldn't find a trace of him in the places where they looked.

What I couldn't understand was why the newspaper hadn't had any stories about him being so disagreeable and all of the guns that were supposed to have been attempted to be smuggled to him before that. That sounds to me like it would have been real news, and would have sold a lot of papers.

But they had just run all that stuff about how cool and calm Wagner appeared, and how he was smiling and friendly in court, and shook hands with his friends and all, and hadn't said a word about him being so blamed mean until after the escape took place.

Right after the incident where some prisoners got one of the cell doors torn down and tried to use it as a battering ram to break out a window with, which I had seen part of, the county had hired extra guards to work in the daytime as well as at night.

But where were those extra guards when the jailbreak took place?

According to the story, one of them was standing outside the jail when Wagner and Davenport came out, and he even claimed he exchanged shots with them, and that they grabbed a woman who was standing there and used her as a shield to keep him from shooting them.

But then, he said, they walked off down the road, and he didn't say anything about them taking the woman with them, and he never was able to hit one of them, shooting all his bullets at them.

And the jailers wife, who claimed she emptied a revolver shooting at Wagner, and the trustee, who said he got a rifle and run after them, shooting all the way, while Wagner and Davenport just strolled along, sort of nonchalantly, 100 yards or so, crawled under a fence and disappeared into the woods, without either of them getting a scratch from all that lead that was whizzing all around them .... well, it just didn't seem to hold as much water as a gunnysack, at least to a lot of people who thought about what they read.

The prevailing opinion, which never did get printed as far as I know, was that somebody goofed and let Wagner and the others get away, and that they were now trying to cover that up by telling a lot of exciting details that maybe only happened in their minds.

Slip Simpson come by where I was working on my truck and said that he had just stopped by the newspaper office to find out if there was anything new on the Wagner escape, and that there wasn't, but the girl at the desk said that two other people had been in that day to ask the same thing.

So when the newspaper came out that evening, that was the story they had.

"Interest In Fate of Wagner Is Still At High Pitch In City," the headline ran.

"Many are of the opinion that Kinnie Wagner has made a safe get-away from his pursuers.

"There is yet widespread interest in the outcome of the search for the desperate fugitive and numberless inquiries are being made at the Times office regarding the latest developments in the manhunt."

From what Slip said, he was the third one that day, and since he was there just at press time, I figured the "numberless" comment was a little bit of an exaggeration, but lots of folks were still interested all right.

You have to expect a newspaper to go on that way. It makes them feel like the folks who read it feel like they are important and busy and all such as that, and that is what keeps them going.

Some folks like to think that newspapers always get rich, but that is an opinion that is open for debate. I don't think I ever saw a rich newspaperman. They like to pretend that they are rich, and some of them go around acting as if they are, but I have noticed that they go to the bank a lot, and to the loan desk rather than the deposit counter.

After all, what can you expect from people who are in a business …the only one in the world I know of, where they have to design, build, manufacture, and market a brand new product every day?

If you make waste cans for a living, you can build a bunch of them up, and then spend your time selling them. Even after a week or a month or even longer, the waste can is still a waste can, and is just as much in demand as it was the first day it was offered for sale.

But if you manufacture a newspaper for a living, you only have a few hours to sell out all copies you have printed and then you have to start all over again, and make up a new one, from front page to back, with new stuff in it all the way. And nobody wants to buy yesterday's newspaper, even at a bargain price.

I have heard that there are some little old ladies around who have pet canaries, and they get old newspapers sometimes to line their bird cages with. And I guess if you have to start a lot of fires, you might have some use for them, or if you need to clean up after dogs, or wrap fish. But the market is NOT what you might call a bullmarket for a newspaperman's leftover stock, so you can't blame them for trying to act a bit uppity if that will increase their per copy sales, or for using words that might be sort of adding a bit of gild to the lily now and again.

"Interest was at an extra high pitch yesterday when practically everyone thought some clue would be found, but all were disappointed for no trace whatever was found of the slayer. Officers are at a loss as to the whereabouts of Wagner. Erroneous reports saying that Wagner has been seen here and there for the past 3 days and nights have in large measure added to the confusion of officers and citizens combing the country. Some have responded to messages saying that Wagner has been seen at a certain place but nothing of foundational value has been obtained. Possemen are returning from the hunt exhausted while others are filling their places and the hunt is still on with officers intent on the recapture of the criminals."

Sheriff Joe Thomas had deputized about everybody he could find, except for me, and I had made it a point to be busy elsewhere whenever he came around.

Up to that point, that is.

But he come up on me while I was working on my truck engine, and I didn't see him until it was too late.

"Potter," he said, and I jumped so hard I bumped my head on the blamed engine cover, which I had propped up so I could get to it better.

"Hello, Joe," I answered, rubbing my head where I had hit it.

"You haven't been in on the manhunt yet, have you?" the sheriff asked, and I had to admit that I had not.

"Well, I got a special assignment for you," he announced. "You are hereby deputized. I want you to go to Norton, Virginia, and check out a story for me."

I always thought they were supposed to swear you in or something, but nothing like that happened at all.

The sheriff just told me that the county would pay my gas expense and pay me a per diem rate to go on the trip and take a couple of other deputies with me.

"Why send me?" I asked him. "Looks like you'd want your regular deputies to go in one of the regular police cars."

"Got them all too busy," he said. "I am sending one regular deputy along, and another special deputy, like you. This is supposed to be a good tip, and Wagner may be still over there, ready to shoot it out, so we don't want to take chances.

"On the other hand, I can't afford to get my force here spread too thin, because he may still be close around here and we could yet flush him out. I'm afraid that if that is so, he may come out with both guns blazing, and I will need all the men I can get right here.

"But we have a good tip that Wagner and three others are said to have been seen and recognized. You can be there in two or three hours, and find out for sure."

Two or three hours, my foot, I thought to myself. I'd have to blamed near fly over them narrow mountain roads to get there as quick as all that. Norton was a good half-day's drive, and the sheriff knew that as well as I did.

"Who are you sending with me?" I asked, knowing that I was caught and there wasn't any easy way to get out of it.

"I thought about sending Groseclose," the sheriff said, "but he is never around when I need him, for some reason. So I'm going to let Billets and the Hughes boy go along with you."

Avery Billets was an older man, but he had a good reputation and had been a deputy sheriff for several years. I had seen him in marksmanship contests a time or two, and knew that he could give a very good account of himself if it came to using a pistol.

Hughes was new to me. As it turned out, I decided it might be best to keep it that way. He was a young fellow, a little on the smart-aleck side, and too cocky to be much good for anything else.

Billets and I put him in the backseat where he could talk to himself all he wanted, and we climbed in the front and headed off toward Norton, 60 miles away as the crow flies, and double that by mountain road, especially in the dark, which it would be in about an hour.

The road to Norton, Virginia, in those days was a long, narrow, winding mountain trail, still unpaved in a good many stretches that covered difficult miles.

From Kingsport over to Gate City, it wasn't so bad. Heavy traffic coming out of the Virginia hills to the Eastman plant and other Kingsport industrial firms, either as workers or as job seekers, had required that good roads be constructed, and new bridges built, so that part of it was just fine.

But after you left Gate City, which the old timers used to call Estilville, and some still do, the roads got narrower and curvier. Up through the area past Clinchport and Duffield, I was careful to drive in the middle of the road, because there wasn't any other traffic and I knew I would be able to see headlights of another car coming toward me in time to pull over as best I could. Crossing Powell Mountain was even worse.

There were no shoulders on the roadway, and in many places there was a sheer drop right down the side of the mountain.

I got so tired of turning and twisting around them blamed hairpin curves I was halfway sorry I had agreed to come.

We only met two other cars and one truck on the way over there and didn't have any trouble getting by either of them because one of them was in Big Stone Gap and the other two between there and Appalachia, which is only a couple of miles on up the road.

They are both coal miners' towns, but they are as different as day and night. Appalachia is where the miners live and hang out, and Big Stone Gap is where the bosses live.

Big Stone Gap is clean and orderly, peaceful and nice. Appalachia is dirty and sprawling, always looking for a fight or some other fun.

There are often knifings and shootings and fights and occasional killings in Appalachia, but if such a thing happens in Big Stone, the cops there load it up in a police car and haul it up the road to Appalachia and blame them with it.

There is a big old hotel at Appalachia where visiting sales folk and other transient business people stay, and a good many of them are young and attractive and of the female gender, which has caused a good bit of talk in certain circles, but which I can not speak of first hand with any knowledgeable authority, on account of having never frequented said establishment, either as a guest or patron, if there is any difference.

Big Stone, on the other hand, wouldn't allow such crass establishments in their town, and so the bigwigs who lived there had to avail themselves of the facilities two miles up the road, in Appalachia, which, it was said, they did on a regular basis.

That way, the preachers at the Big Stone churches could rant and rave all they wanted about the sin city right up the road, just as long as they didn't catch on or mention that the target of their sermons existed mainly because of the support and patronage of those smug-looking community pillars who sat in the congregation, doing their best to appear righteous and upstanding, and as innocent as newborn babes.

We got to talking about Kinnie Wagner and the other escapees as we rattled along the mountain roads, which was a natural conversation, seeing as how we might possibly run into them over there some place.

Young Hughes was sure that we would do so.

Billets and I both had serious doubts about that, because we had already heard so many different stories about Wagner and the others and where they were and all that any of them were any place at all within range of being arrested.

"They're over there!" Hughes declared. "And I'm going to get them!"

He had a big, long-barreled pistol strapped on his side and was toting a shotgun, which he wanted to hold onto, but which I insisted that he put down on the floorboards of the car.

He was riding in the back seat, right behind me, and blamed if I was going to allow some nervous kid who was keeping his courage up by talking big to hold a shotgun in his hands when he was riding behind me going over a bumpy road like we were!

Billets just kind of grinned to himself and didn't say much, but I got to sort of drawing Hughes out on the subject.

"The man who gets Wagner is going to make a name fer hisself," the youngster declared.

139

"I been practicing with this old pistol for a whole year now, and I kin shoot just as good as HE kin, I'll bet you. Why, I kin hit a tin can 9 times out of 10 at a hundred feet!

"And I kin draw fast, too. That could be mighty important, you know. In a desp'rt situation. The sheriff hisself says I am as good a shot as enybody on the force! Why, if we find them crimminels holed up over ther in Norton, I'll blast 'em out. I ain't a bit skeered."

He kept cleaning the gun or otherwise checking it over until I got a mite nervous thinking about him handling it all the time while he was setting right behind me.

I felt a lot better when he would occasionally slide over to the other side of the back seat and try to talk to Billets, but Billets, blame him, just ignored him, so pretty soon he would come scooting back over to my side and talk some more.

"When we get there, you fellers kin do the talking, but if it comes to a shootout, you just back my play," he declared.

"I'll stand right up and shoot it out with all of them if I have to.

"Kinnie Wagner might be a deadly shot and all like that, but he ain't never gone up against ME."

I got plumb tired of hearing him brag and blow that way and finally got to thinking about what I could do to hush him up.

We were nearly up the mountain to Norton when it hit me. I believe Billets thought of it about the same time, because he suddenly looked at me and grinned.

Just as we come rolling down the steep hill into town, I reached up and cut the switch off and yelled, "There they are!"

I cut the switch back on just as I said it, and you never heard such a back-fire as that old car let out! In the back seat, young Hughes grabbed for his pistol, dropped it and lost it, and ducked down as low in the floorboards as he could get, whimpering like a puppy.

It was dark, of course, and that was the only thing that saved the Hughes boy from a fatal case of embarrassment.

As it was, he felt and fumbled around down there on the floorboards of the back seat for some time after he caught on to what had happened, pretending that he had dropped something and was hunting for it in the dark.

Billets and I were tempted to ride him some about his plans to shoot it out with Wagner, but after having heard how pitifully he whimpered and moaned when he thought that backfire was a gunshot, we just didn't have the heart to do it.

We got into Norton about 11 o'clock that night, tired and weary from the long ride. I don't know why it is, but driving over mountain roads at night seems farther than it does in the daylight. You'd think it would be the other way, because after dark there's not nearly as much to look at, just the road in the headlight's beam in front of you, and the few things you can see a glimpse of now and again.

But in the daytime, you can see houses and mountains and people and livestock and dogs and cats and sometimes pretty girls and other cars and trucks and farm wagons and all sorts of things, and your eyes are kept busy just trying to watch the road instead of a hundred other things they'd rather look at.

Why it should be that looking at so little, like you do at night, should be so much more tiresome than looking at lots of things, I never could understand, but it seems to work that way.

Within an hour, we had already found out that we had driven all that way in the dark on another wild goose chase, and that if Wagner and the others had been there, they were long, long gone.

What had happened, as nearly as we could find out, was that four men had driven into the town in a Ford roadster late on Friday night.

They had stopped there to get something to eat, and one of the men, a tall, good-looking fellow in his early twenties, had tried to get a check cashed at the hotel.

The hotel clerk had apologized, but, because the man did not provide sufficient identification, would not cash the check, which I figured was what you might call a prudent move.

The young man seemed irritated at the refusal, and sort of stormed out of the hotel, his three companions with him.

The clerk got a mite nervous because of the young man's attitude, which seemed to him to be one of threatening menace.

One of the hotel guests happened into the lobby about that time, and, when the clerk told him of the incident, the guest, who had passed through Kingsport just after the spectacular escape, concluded that it may have been Wagner.

Stories like that always get elaborated, and by the time we got there to check it out, it had grown a whole set of facts that weren't true as far as we could find out.

It was being claimed that Wagner and the others had told a friend of the young shooter all about their escape, and how they had planned it, executed it, and what they were going to do now that they had

141

gotten away, but we never did find anybody who admitted to being that friend.

It was also claimed that they abandoned the Ford and left town on a freight train, but we couldn't find any trace of the car, and I sure wasn't inclined to believe that they took the blamed thing with them. We went back to the car and climbed in it and got a few hours of restless sleep, if you can call fitful dozing sleep.

Then, after eating breakfast at a restaurant there, we headed down the long road back to Kingsport. By the time we pulled back into Kingsport, we were all three pretty well tuckered out.

I had done all the driving, of course, seeing as how it was my car we were in, and besides that, I figured Billets was too old to do much driving and Hughes was too much the other way, at least in MY car, so I should have been more worn out than the others.

But Billets had started nodding a few miles out of Norton, his head sort of drooping down so his chin could rest on his breastbone, and he gradually drifted off into a fitful sleep.

Before we were halfway up the first mountain, he had leaned back against the car door and was peacefully snoring away.

Hughes didn't sleep, I don't think, but he sat there in the back seat and sulked over the trick we had pulled on him with that backfire just when he was doing so much bragging about how he was going to shoot it out with the desperados if we saw them.

It was his pride that had gotten bruised, and I kind of regretted that we had done it, because he looked to me to be the kind of fool that carries a grudge, and I have enough of those in my circle of acquaintances already.

On our arrival in town, we drove up to the police station on Main Street and called the sheriff in Blountville, to report.

He took our failure to discover anything tangible as a matter of course, but told me that he had a mighty good lead at the moment, having just found out that Wagner was definitely in Johnson City, and that he was getting ready to go over there himself and see to it in person.

"This time, I've got the goods," he told me. "A real reliable source gave me this information."

Well, I wished him luck and hung up, about half way disgusted. If he had known all along that the trip to Norton was so blamed useless, he could of at least let me wait until morning to drive all that way and not have to fight all them mountain curves in the dark!

As it turned out, his tip about Wagner being in Johnson City was just as groundless as the Norton story. He and the Johnson City chief of police and a dozen or so officers all surrounded this house where they thought Wagner was hiding, and finally banged on the door and demanded that he come out, and then went in and searched the place, but all they found was a tall, skinny young man and his Ma, back in the kitchen, breaking and stringing green beans.

The boy had just come home from working on a farm, and somebody had seen him go into the house carrying a big bundle, which they thought was clothes or something and maybe guns, but it was only green beans, which he had been working and took home to his Ma .... anyway, some idiot thought it was Wagner, but, of course, it wasn't.

Opinion was about evenly divided in Kingsport as to whether Wagner was hiding out someplace near or had already made himself long gone from the entire region.

Wagner had a flock of relatives in and around both Kingsport and Scott County, and if he had been planning to hideout, I figured that was the most likely place to look for him, if they really wanted to find him.

But I knew of a dozen or more such places that they never checked, although several of the folks involved in the searching posses knew about them just as well as I did. Then, to make matters even more confused, we got word that there had just been a massive jailbreak down at Greeneville, Tennessee, and 40 to 50 desperate, hardened killers had escaped and were going to blast their way through to the Virginia line, right through Kingsport, shooting at anybody or anything that got in their way.

As it turned out, that was what you might call exaggerated considerably more than somewhat.

There had been a jailbreak alright, and some of the prisoners who escaped were being held on suspicion of murder. But there were only18 of them, not half a hundred or so like we had first heard.

Two of the escapees were being held as murder suspects in the shotgun killing of a deputy sheriff who had got a bit too close to a moonshine still a few months earlier, and I guess that's where the hardened killer talk got started from.

At any rate, Greene County was all up in arms and having the same blamed kind of posse search that had been going on around Kingsport and Bristol for the past few days, and they didn't have much more luck at it than we did.

Some folks claimed later that all 18 of the jailbirds just walked out of the jail, due to the carelessness of a guard who left a door unlocked. They had climbed aboard a freight train that was standing on the tracks around back of the building, and rode all the way to Cincinnati, which is as good a place for jail prisoners to go as any other I can think of.

But it caused a lot more excitement in town.

There was even talk that Kinnie Wagner had somehow managed to get down to Greeneville and pull off that escape as well.

Some folks claimed that he was planning to travel all around the country, busting prisoners out of jails, just to make it more impossible to get caught himself.

The idea there was, you see, that the more desperate jailbirds that got out, the busier the law would be trying to herd them all back up again, and the easier it would be for a smart man to get lost in the shuffle.

It was silly when you thought about it.

An escaped prisoner who has just broken out of jail wants just one thing .... that is to get as far away from his pursuers as he can get. And having more prisoners loose at the same time would only mean that more and more law would be out looking, and that would make it harder to get through them, and get away, which would be the main goal in any case.

Besides that, it would be down-right stupid for an escaped desperado to fool around breaking other prisoners out of jail, because the jail is where sheriffs and deputies hang out most of the time, and that would be like trying to crawl under a hornet's nest without getting stung. But some folks believe what they WANT to believe, not what they OUGHT to believe, which is why we've got so many different brands of religions, I figure.

That also may be the reason that some men chase around after other men's wives.

The rumors and talk brought a lot more folks to town, though, and the cars were parked everywhere, as the curious citizenry chased around after the latest gossip or "reported" information.

It got so bad you couldn't find a place to park on Broad Street at all. There were even a couple of cars parked up on the greenway in the middle of the street, and the police had to get a wrecker and tow them off.

So the merchants who had stores along there got upset over it, figuring that all those cars were keeping their customers from getting to their stores, and they started talking about getting the city to pass some kind of a law to regulate parking in Kingsport, or put an hour limit on it at least.

The rumors died down after that, but ever now and again you'd still hear talk about how Kinnie Wagner was hiding out close around town.

They arrested Wagner's younger brother and tried him on a charge of trying to smuggle arms to the prisoner while he was in Blountville jail...convicted him of it, too, and sentenced him to a year and a day at Brushy Mountain state prison.

I didn't know anyone on the jury, and didn't attend any of the trial, so I couldn't say as how I had formed an opinion on whether he was guilty or not, but a whole lot of folks felt that he was not, and even if he was, he only did what a brother might be expected to do, and it was down right underhanded of the courts and the law to make a big issue out of it.

"They're just taking it out on him because Kinnie got away," folks said.

"And the main reason HE got away is that they was afraid of him, and knew that he could outshoot all of them put together, so they give him a good head start before they began trying to catch him, and then they went in the opposite direction from the way they knew he had gone, just to keep from taking chances."

Young Wagner, looking like a miniature of the wanted man, being short and slight, where his now infamous brother was tall and robust, had the same general features and bearing as the pistol artist now so desperately wanted by the police.

But he did not have just the same sort of defiant swagger that officers had come to resent so much in the older and taller brother, and he seemed to have a habit of keeping his mouth shut instead of talking about anything at all.

The newspaper had run so blamed much stuff about the "imminent capture" and all that it got to be downright embarrassing for them, and they quit printing a word about all the rumors that were still cropping up every few days.

When folks started kidding the editor of the paper about that, he got mad and went to Riverside Hospital, claiming he had appendicitis, to get away from all that kind of stuff.

You see, the year before, he had complained of a bad pain in his lower right-hand side, and it had been diagnosed as appendix trouble, but the pain had stopped right after that and there had been no need for an operation.

So he knew how to describe all the symptoms and such again, and did so in detail, figuring that they would keep him a few days and he could stay away from all the wise-acres around town who had been giving him so much discomfort.

There is nothing like a little sick spell to make folks forget about plaguing you about something, and a hospital is about the last place in the world where any smart-aleck will follow you, just to keep on being obnoxious.

But he described the symptoms in so much detail that the young surgeon on duty took it all serious, and before the editor knew what was taking place, a cone of ether was slapped over his nose, and he awoke four hours later with a real pain in his side, this one caused by the surgeon's knife.

He was so blamed mad over it that he refused to see any visitors at all during the entire time he had to be kept in the hospital, and even after that, there were some people he wouldn't speak to for a couple of years.

I never did find out for sure, but I suspected that he blamed it all on Kinnie Wagner, and his legendary escape from the Sullivan County jail.

Kinnie Wagner's Final Escape

World War I, or "the BIG war" as we called it then, had been over for nearly a decade, but many of the fellows who had been participants in it, however unwilling, retained very strong memories and feelings from their European visitation.

Callahan was no exception.

Although not wounded, gassed, nor "shell-shocked", Callahan had an experience while in France that was to remain with him all of his days.

While stationed near Paris, he was granted a week's leave, a furlough, for what was much later to be called "Rest and Recreation".

Not able to speak the language, Callahan nevertheless determined to enjoy himself, and found a room in a hotel with a dining room that had a reputation for serving wonderful food.

And he enjoyed it, too, although he feared he might have a lot of trouble making the waiter understand his orders, and finally decided that he would simply point to pictures of various dishes that were printed on the menu as a way of placing his order.

Callahan liked his privacy, especially because he could not engage in conversation with people he could not speak understandably with, so he wanted to get a table by himself.

But the very first night, he found himself in a small room sharing a table with a Frenchman who rose, bowed, and said, "Bon appetit."

Annoyed, but not to be outdone, Callahan bowed and said, "Callahan".

This performance lasted for nearly the entire week of Callahan's furlough. Every night the waiter escorted Callahan to the same little room, which was always occupied by the same Frenchman, who rose and bowed, saying "Bon Appetit" as he had that very first time.

Callahan, grimly determined not to be outdone, would return the bow and again say, "Callahan", but he seethed at the ignominy of it all.

One night he could no longer keep his temper.

"I'm glad my leave is almost over," he told an Englishman he happened to meet.

"That guy Bon Appetit is driving me crazy. Every night, he introduces himself to me all over again. I'm sick of it."

"But you don't understand," the Englishman said.

"That's not his name. Bon Appetit is a French expression meaning "I wish you a pleasant meal".

"Is that so?" Callahan said. "Well I'll be dogged." That evening he hurried to the dining room so he could get there first, and waited for the Frenchman to arrive.

As soon as the man came into the room, Callahan jumped up, bowed, and said, "Bon Appetit!" determined to pay back his misunderstood dining companion of so many days.

The Frenchman smiled broadly, and returned the bow.

"Callahan!" he replied.

After his escape from the Sullivan County Jail, the search for Kinnie Wagner continued for weeks, even months, but proved to be unfruitful. There were rumors a-plenty.

I heard a lot of them, and I'm sure the law officers must have known all about them as well, about how Kinnie was staying at this house or that house, visiting this relative or that friend, but no arrest was made. A couple of his relatives had bragged to me that he was staying with them now and then, but another one swore that Kinnie had made his way down to old Mexico, and was a deputy sheriff down there.

The weeks turned into months, and the months dragged into a year, before the next news of the young desperado became known.

And it wasn't Tennessee, Virginia or Mississippi where it took place, nor Mexico, either, but in Texarkana, Arkansas.

As luck would have it, I was at the newspaper office that day, helping Charley Houser unload a stack of newsprint I had delivered to him from their warehouse.

The paper they used came in large sheets in those days, not in the big, heavy rolls that were used later on what is called "web" presses; the sheet-fed newspaper press of those early years printed two pages at a time, work-and-turn, and there was a folding machine that took two sheets at a time and folded them twice to make a eight page newspaper section out of them.

When the press was running, a "printers-devil", usually a boy about twelve years old, carried stacks of the big flat sheets up to the feeder, where the pressman, in this case, Charley, fed them through the machine to print a-side-at-a-time.

We had just unloaded my truck and finished stacking the paper on a skid near the press, which Charley called a "Babcock Flatbed" when this guy who worked in the news office came running in through the door to the press room, hollering for Charley.

"What'cha want?" Charley asked. "I'm standin' right here."

148

His stubby black pipe was stuck tightly between his teeth, but thrust up at a jaunty angle that seemed to say he was in no mood to be yelled at, and might take retaliatory action.

"We got to get out an extra," the breathless man said. "They just got Kinnie Wagner!"

Well, Charley's expression suddenly said, that was different. Why didn't you say so in the first place?

I was quickly forgotten in the mad scramble that followed.

Charley immediately began cleaning the press, checking it over to see that it was ready to run. The excited man ran back through the door into the news department, and I followed along, casually, to find out what was going on.

The clatter and clang of the wire machine could be heard as soon as I got through the door.

A couple of men were trying to talk on telephones, asking questions and scribbling down notes as rapidly as they could. The excitable fellow, now seated at a desk, was shuffling through back copies of the newspaper from more than a year ago, trying to note down facts that had been printed when Wagner made his now-famous escape from Blountville Jail.

I could see the date on the old paper: July 10, 1925.

It was now August 18,1926. The young desperado had been on the run, avoiding capture, for more than thirteen months.

The way I got the story, gathered from news reports and a lot of talk by town folk, was something like the following:

Kinnie had roamed through Virginia and Tennessee, and had even gone back down to Mississippi, which I thought was kind of foolhardy, due to the fact that he was wanted for murder there; making his way toward eventual escape to Mexico, where he could live out his days as a cowboy.

He made it to Arkansas, and found occasional work there as a farmhand, trying to gain enough cash to stand him in good stead when he finally made it across the border.

But farmhand work is lonely and rough, muscles grow taut and nerves do too.

Kinnie found that Sunday afternoons, his only time off, became times to pack in all the talk and visiting and associating with others as completely as he could.

It was on one such afternoon that he happened to walk up to a barn in the backcountry southeast of Texarkana.

149

According to reports by witnesses, a group of men were there, laughing and talking and playing cards. They were drinking moonshine whiskey, too.

"Who are you?" one of the men asked the tall young stranger.

"My name is Harry Logan", Kinnie declared. He may have taken that alias from the once-infamous East Tennessee bad man Harvey Logan, notorious for his shooting exploits a half century earlier.

The men who were gathered in the barn were a rough bunch, led by two local scoundrels known as the "Carper Brothers".

William and Sam Carper were currently hiding out from the law, for they were suspects in the murder of the County Sheriff Wade Barber, who had been shot down from ambush sometime earlier.

Barber's wife, Lily, had been given the star her late husband had worn and was asked by the sympathetic County Judge to finish out the Sheriff's term. After thinking it over, she had agreed to take the job and thus became one of Arkansas' first women law officers.

"Come on in, Logan," the big man said. "We need some new blood in this here card game."

The whiskey flowed freely as the jugs were passed around.

Kinnie wasn't used to doing much drinking, but he took his turn with the fiery liquid when it was passed to him.

He got into the card game and soon began to win hand after hand.

One of the Carper brothers, William, was losing heavily. His face developed a fierce scowl, and he began to curse and complain about his cards, the barn, and apparently everything else he could think of.

"Aw, cheer up," Kinnie told him. "You're due for a winning hand. Your luck will turn soon."

"A lot YOU know about luck," the disgruntled gambler snorted.

This comment, made unaware to a man who had been lucky enough to shoot it out with at least a dozen men in Mississippi and half that number in Tennessee and escape his pursuers and captors more times than he could remember, went unanswered and ignored.

But just then, a ten year old boy came busting into the barn.

Carper jumped up, grabbed the boy by the shoulder, and spun him around.

"What are YOU doing in here, you little devil?" he roared. "You get the hell out of here right now!"

With that, the burly Carper slapped the youngster, hard, across the mouth.

Kinnie was on his feet instantly.

"Here now," he said, mildly. "If you want to slap somebody around, why don't you try somebody your own size?"

Carper's face flushed bright red. He shoved the boy violently away and made a lunge at Wagner.

Kinnie, accustomed to fist fights and brawls from both his cowboy days and circus work, dodged to one side and sent a rock hard fist slamming into Carper's jaw.

Staggered, but not knocked down, William Carper flailed out with his long arms and began to plummet his opponent with all his might.

Kinnie ducked and dodged, taking most of Carper's blows on his ample shoulders. His piston-like arms shot out hard fists at any opportunity, cutting Carper's lip and smashing hard against his right ear.

Sam Carper, taken by surprise with the suddenness of the fight, leaped to his feet and tried to grab Kinnie from behind, hoping to pin his arms in a bear hug so his brother could make short work of this fierce opponent.

But Kinnie's quick reflexes came to his aid again, and Sam found himself knocked back against the barn's wall, spitting blood and a loose tooth from his smashed mouth.

Trying to get back to his feet, Sam Carper's hand pressed against the rough-hewn board of the barn wall. Something brushed against his fingers, and he glanced that way to see a whiffletree or swingletree hanging there below other harness equipment.

Burning with anger and hatred, Carper grabbed the sturdy wooden bar and swung it with all his might against the back of the stranger's head.

"Now, Will!" he shouted. "Kill the Basser!"

William Carper gave a vicious chuckle and jumped forward, ready to destroy his suddenly slack antagonist.

For months after Kinnie Wagner escaped from the Sullivan County Jail and headed for Scott County, Va. while the posse searched in the opposite direction so they danged sure wouldn't run into him, and you couldn't really blame them too much, knowing that he had taken at least one .38 Special pistol from Jailer Barr before he lit out, and knowing what a deadly shot he had recently proved to be and all ... for that time and more, the local newspaper kept on claiming that the young desperado's capture was "imminent".

I think they really believed that the local law would eventually find and arrest the youthful badman, although they were certainly in the minority about that conviction.

Most folks seemed to think that Kinnie would remain hidden for the rest of his life, if he was still in the country. There was talk that he had gone to Mexico and started a new life and was now a law man down there himself.

"Why, it wouldn't surprise me not a'tal I if he got to be a high government official down there," Lester Lucas said. "He's plenty smart, and can ride horses well, and he is a great shot with a gun. Them Mex people admire that kind of talent, and usually make a feller like that into a gener'l or sumpin."

Others said that Wagner was still living in Scott County, hiding out with relatives and commuting to work in a nearby Kentucky coal mine with a couple of Kingsport men. They supposedly drove over on Sunday nights, worked from Monday through Friday, then drove home again for the weekend. Wagner, it was claimed, rode with them from a certain pickup place in Scott County and back again on their return trip.

Now and again, somebody would report seeing the fugitive in town, and Dr. Will Hutchins would leave quickly for Florida.

Dr. Hutchins, a dentist, had cursed Kinnie and spit on him in the hallway of the Kingsport Police Station when the young shooter had first given himself up and was being taken to the Blountville Jail.

Bystanders claimed Kinnie looked the toothpuller in the eye and told him that he would kill him for that someday, but I don't know for sure. I was there, and I know that something of the kind happened, but I understood Wagner to say "You'll regret that someday" or words to that effect. Of course, if he made the threat they now attributed to him, then I suppose the dentist would regret that, sure enough.

At any rate, he left town every time the rumor of Wagner's presence came up, and he stayed away until he was reasonably sure it was safe to return home again.

Cap Galyon, who ran a gasoline station, made a good bit of money off of Doc, always filling up his car's gas tank and keeping it road ready at all times, just in case a quick trip out of town became a pressing demand.

Other stories grew as well, including tales of Wagner's powers with a six gun. Tricks that Tom Mix and Ken Maynard and Tex Blaine had done on the silver screen all soon became a part of the Kinnie

152

Wagner story. To listen to some local folk, he shot back over his shoulder, using a mirror to aim with, and hit the target dead center every time, they said. He could put a bullet into the hole made by a bullet a hundred yards away, they said. He could out-draw, out-shoot and out-smart all the police in the country, they said. I didn't believe a whole lot of it, but the talk sure grew.

Whether he had intended self-defense or cold blooded murder, Kinnie Wagner was rapidly becoming a local folk hero.

And so it went for a year and more. Then, on August 18,1926, sixteen months after the shootout on the banks of the Holston River, the unbelievable happened. A young man walked in to the office of a woman sheriff in Texarkana, Ark.

Sheriff Lily Barber looked at the pile of paperwork on her cluttered desk and sighed deeply.

Since taking over as sheriff, to fulfill the unexpired term of her late husband, Lily had found it a constant struggle to keep ahead of all the demanding details the position of county sheriff entailed. Wade, her murdered husband, had paid little attention to such details.

"It'll all come out in the wash", he had said. "My job is to enforce the law. Let somebody else keep up with the records if they want to."

The county judge, a special friend of Wade's, had gone along with that sort of thinking.

As a result, the records of the county were in poor shape. Nobody could tell, without searching for days among the scattered papers stuffed into file cabinets seemingly at random, whether a warrant had been served at a certain time, or find the arrest record of a local individual. Wade had compensated with his remarkable memory. He never forgot a detail, a face, or a friend.

He could always bring to mind, after a bit of thinking, who had been arrested for what, who had been under suspicion, and what other actions had been taken.

Lily had no such memory, nor did she have the long experience Wade had known. Her only familiarity with the job of law enforcement and sheriff had been through Wade's occasional talking about his work, and how he had done certain things.

Yet, when the judge had offered her the opportunity to take over Wade's job until the term expired, Lily had decided to accept the challenge. Wade's murderer was still at large, and, by controlling the office of sheriff, there was a good chance she could bring that vicious killer to justice.

The paperwork, however, was something she had failed to bargain for.

Actually, Lily's efforts had brought great improvement to the office, even though she failed to realize that fact. She had established a filing system that was fairly workable, and had made some strides toward organizing the entire office. Sunday afternoons, she had found, gave her opportunity to study over her files and records and put more of the vital material in a safe place.

She looked up at the sound of the office door opening. Deputy George Greene's head appeared.

"Sheriff Lily, there's a young man here who insists on seeing you," Greene said.

Lily sighed again. The paperwork would have to wait a while longer.

"Alright, George," she said. "Let him come in."

Seconds later, a tall youth with wavy hair appeared in the doorway.

"You the sheriff, M'am?" he asked.

"Yes. What can I do for you?"

"Well, M'am," the lanky visitor drawled in a mellow, southern-mountain voice, "I reckon I want to surrender myself to you. I think I just killed two men."

"What?" The sheriff was suddenly alert and all attention.

"Where did this happen. Who were they? Who are you?"

"I'm Harry Logan. I think I must have shot the two Carper brothers. We were playing cards at this old barn, out in the country a piece, and one of them started a fight with me. The other one hit me in the head with a swingletree he grabbed off the wall, and knocked me out.

"I don't know just what happened, to tell the truth. When I come to myself, my gun was lying beside me and these two Carper brothers were layin' there dead. They'd been shot, and with my gun. So I reckon I must have done it, although I truly can't remember it."

"Carper?" Lily Barber was on the edge of her chair now. "Sam Carper? And his brother William?"

"Yes M'am," the young man admitted. "That's the men. I had never met them before today, and I don't really know them. We were playing cards and drinkin' some, then this fight started."

"I've been trying to find them for months," Sheriff Barber declared.

"I'm pretty sure they are the men who killed my husband. They have been accused of robbing people and other crimes."

She called Deputy Greene.

"This man is turning himself in," she said. "We'll have to hold him until we can see if the judge wants to try him for killing those Carpers. Actually, he may have done the state a big favor by killing them, but the judge will have to decide about that.

"Lock him up, Greene, while I go investigate what he told me."

"I'm sorry, Harry Logan, but we'll have to hold you until we find out more."

Had it not been for an itinerant cowboy, arrested earlier for public drunkenness and now sobering up in a jail cell, "Harry Logan" might well have stood trial for the dual killings of the Carper Brothers, and there is a fine chance that, with a self defense plea, he might have been acquitted.

But fate, in the guise of that inebriated cowpuncher was to take a hand.

"Here's your cell, Harry Logan," the Deputy declared, unlocking the door of steel rods. "In you go."

"Hey, Shurff," the drunk cowboy called, "Where'd ya get that Harry Logan stuff? That ain't no Harry Logan you got there. That there's Kinnie Wagner, the best shot in three states! I used to work wiff him as a cowboy in th'circus, and I know him well. That's ol' Kinnie, alright!" Faced with this unexpected recognition, the young desperado admitted his identity and the news wires were soon humming all across the land.

"Kinnie Wagner Captured" they screamed. "Two Gun Desperado, Kills Two More Men in Card Game Fight."

Sheriff Barber, anxious to learn the full truth, once again sent for the prisoner and interviewed him privately.

"Young man," she said, "I understand that you have been convicted of two murders in Tennessee and sentenced to be electrocuted. And Mississippi has a warrant out for your arrest on another murder charge. There's even a thousand dollar reward for you, dead or alive. Now, I may have to bring double murder charges against you for killing the Carper Brothers, even though they were also wanted men.

"I've got to decide whether to send you back to Tennessee to the electric chair or let Mississippi have you for trial, or keep you for trial here.

"I'd like to know your side of things. That might help me make the decision."

"Alright, M'am," Kinnie said. "I'll tell you the full, true story. Then you can decide what is best for you to do.

"I was born in Scott County, Virginia, near a little place called Speers Ferry, in 1903.

"When I was a youngster, my mother died. I grieved over her for a long, long time. I still miss her, to tell the truth.

"My father married again, and my stepmother is a fine woman, but I was still always very lonely and sad. I worked as a rural mail carrier some, delivering the mail on horseback, but at last I just couldn't stand staying at home, and I left to make my own way in the world.

"I joined up with a circus, and traveled with them for some time. I worked as a cowboy with them, and sometimes, I'd take time off and work on a real ranch out west when we were out that way. I learned to shoot pretty well, although I had been able to shoot a rifle since I was just a little boy. I used to hunt rabbits and squirrels as a youngster.

"The circus life was exciting, and we traveled all over the country. I enjoyed riding the horses and shooting at targets and such, putting on a show for the customers.

"Last year, we were in winter quarters down in Leaksville, Mississippi.

"There wasn't much to do, so I took a job at a lumber mill near there.

"After working awhile, I found out that the county sheriff down there was a terrible crook. He owned most of the gin mills and dance halls and roadhouses and bootleg joints, and took a pay-off from the ones he didn't own.

"If anyone was robbed, or a woman raped, or somebody murdered or cheated in a crooked gambling game, nothing much ever was done about it, for the law, under that sheriff, was on the side of the criminal in many cases.

"I made a remark about what a sorry, low-down sheriff that man was, and said I hoped that someday, someone would tell the true story about what kind of a man he was.

"Well, the sheriff found out what I'd said. He sent me word that I'd better keep my big mouth shut, and that I was already in trouble.

"He had his son, who was a deputy, plant a watch in my pocket and then report that it had been stolen.

"The Sheriff then began to search people for the stolen watch, and I was one of the first he searched. He found the watch ... I'd never seen it before, and arrested me for theft. They locked me up in jail.

"That was on Christmas eve, 1924. 1 spent a cold night looking through the bars of a high window. The next morning, a deputy brought me some breakfast ... mush, it was...and walked off, leaving the door of my cell unlocked!

"I walked right out the door and went to the house where I'd been staying to get my clothes and leave, planning to go as far away from that crooked place as I could.

"But while I was there, the sheriff and all his men surrounded the house and yelled for me to come out. Before I could do anything, they began to shoot. They shot that house up like nothing you've ever seen. Bullets were crashing through all the windows and doors and even the thin walls. I lay down on the floor to keep from being riddled, and even then, I got a crease on one shoulder from one that came too close.

"I lay still and very quiet, trying to not make a move or a sound. They quit shooting after a long time, and I heard the sheriff order someone to 'Go in there and drag him out'.

"I had stuck my gun in my belt when I started to pack my clothes, so it was quickly in my hand.

"A deputy came through the door, shading his eyes against the pistol smoke that floated through the room.

"He saw me and started toward me, then he realized that I was still alive and he threw up his pistol and clicked the hammer back, ready to blast my head off.

"I rolled to one side as he fired, and snapped a shot off at him as I rolled. I didn't miss. My bullet went right between his eyes, and he pitched forward, dead.

"It was only then that I realized it was the sheriff's son, the one who had planted the watch on me and started all this trouble.

"I grabbed a handful of clothes and ran out the back door. There was a horse tethered to a fence post there, and I jumped on him and rode away. There was no saddle, but I was used to bareback riding from the circus work, and I kept him going at top speed until we were far from the scene of the shooting.

"Well, I rode that ol' horse all the way to Tennessee during the next few days. We'd stop at night and I'd sleep under a tree while he grazed on the lush green grass in the fields. I kept him hobbled so he wouldn't run away.

"Once in Tennessee, I worked at different day jobs here and there, making my way toward the Virginia line and home. I got to Kingsport in April. That town is just across the Virginia state line from my home county, and I had lots of friends and relatives around there.

"I sent word to my younger sister that I was there, and that I would like to see her. She sent word back that she and one of my girl cousins would meet me down on the Holston River just west of town, on Monday, the day after Easter, 1925.

"I had already heard that the Sheriff of Greene County, Mississippi, had put up a thousand dollar reward for me, dead or alive, which he claimed was donated by the people of Leaksville. I know that couldn't have been so, for the people of Leaksville never had a hundred dollars between them, much less a thousand. He put it up himself, for revenge, hoping that somebody would kill me and save him the trouble of trying to hunt me down.

"I met my sister and cousin and a friend of mine on the river bank, and we were enjoying visiting with each other. Then, suddenly, one of the girls, my cousin I think it was, looked up and said: "What in the world are those men doing with those guns?"

"I glanced up and saw two men, guns drawn, coming across the field toward the river.

"I glanced to the right, and there was another gunman up there, starting down the river bank toward me.

"I looked quickly to the left and saw a fourth man starting up the river bank from that direction. He had his gun drawn, too.

"Suddenly, one of them fired a shot.

"I shoved my sister and my cousin down on the ground and jumped behind a tree, pulling out my guns as I did so.

"Bullets were suddenly flying around my head from three directions. One of them chipped a hunk of bark out of the sycamore tree I stood behind. I threw up my gun, took quick aim, and fired. One of the men pitched forward and lay still.

"I turned and shot toward the man coming up the river toward me. He, too, fell over in his tracks. "Then I shot toward the man who was starting down the river. He fell, also, and lay still.

"I started to aim at the fourth man, but he was running away, his back toward me. I never shot a man in the back, and never intend to, so I let him go. But I knew I was in real trouble by that time.

"A boy on a horse came by, and I jumped up and grabbed the bridle.

158

"I need your horse," I yelled at him. "I didn't realize I was still waving the gun around in my hand. I must have scared the kid half to death, but I didn't mean to. He slid off the horse and ran away. I swung up on the big animal's back and jerked the reins around, kicking him into a gallop and raced toward the railroad underpass and the high hill beyond, the last ridge that stood between me and my native Virginia.

"I got away, but it was a tough flight. The horse grew winded by the time we got to the top of the high ridge, and I turned him loose, knowing that he would eventually find his way home and back to his master. I ran and slid and hurried down the hill toward the river, which runs from Virginia into Tennessee, and I dodged along the banks, looking for a place to cross.

"They must have organized a posse very quickly, for I soon heard shouts of men and barking of dogs. They were coming after me!   "I dropped down into the waist deep water and waded along the bank, still trying to find a shallow place to cross. Men and dogs suddenly came racing down the hill toward me, and I ducked down under the river bank, my head hid from their sight by the tall grass and weeds.

"The dogs were baying and barking, following my scent along the way I had come. They lost the trail down the riverbank where I had gotten into the water, and circled around in confusion, trying to pick up a trace.

"It was late evening now, and the sun was setting. Twilight shadows improved my hiding, and I carefully waded along the bank, at last finding a shallow ford where I could easily walk across.

"But the posse was searching on the Virginia side, too. Several times during the early hours of that night, I heard them pass within just a few feet of my quickly chosen hiding places.

"I don't know just how long I ran through the fields and woods. But at last I came to a farm, and there was a barn I could hide in. I slept awhile on the hay, exhausted and out of breath so much I scarcely noticed my torn and bleeding feet.

"I had kicked off my shoes when I got in the water at the river, and had been barefoot ever since.

"My stomach was empty, and hunger pains gnawed fiercely, and at last I went to the house to beg food.

"An elderly woman came to the window in answer to my knock. She gave me food and was kind to me. I told her of the serious trouble I was in, and she said she would pray for me!

"I don't think anyone ever did that before. Her name was Mrs. Sam Rhodes, and she was a widow. Her farm was near Waycross. She told me I should give myself up, before any more killing became necessary, and I resolved to do so.

"'But the officers are out to kill me for that thousand dollars,' I told her. 'I won't surrender to any of them.'

"When daylight came, I walked out of the hollow to a country store at the forks of the road. It was run by a man named Poe. I called out for anyone in the store to come out, that I was Kinnie Wagner and that I wanted to surrender to them.

"A number of men came out on the porch, but only one of them came out to the edge of the woods where I stood.

"'I'm D. R. Poe,' he said. 'I run this store.'

"'I've done all the killing I want to do,' I told him.

"'But I'm not going to surrender to any law officer. They'll kill me for that reward, and for revenge. I'll shoot it out with any number of them, if I have to..'

"I asked Poe if he would take me to the authorities in Gate City, and keep the posse or gangs from mobbing me. But first, I got him to write a letter to my father for me, and one to my sister. I told my sister Ollie that I wanted her to have half the reward and that Mr. Poe was to have the rest I told my father the same thing in the letter to him.

"A fellow I knew, Neil Bussel, came along in his Ford Roadster just then, and Poe flagged him down and asked him to take us to Gate City, which he agreed to do. I gave Poe one of my guns, but kept the other one, just in case a bunch of law officers tried to mob me.

"We got in the Roadster and started for Gate City, but another car met us, about a mile and a half from Moccasin Gap, and it was full of law men. When the driver saw me, he got so scared he didn't know what he was doing, and he smashed his car right into ours. He claimed later that he did it on purpose because he saw me and recognized me, and wrecked the cars to catch me, but that was just HIS story. I don't think he meant to do any such a thing. I think he got so scared he didn't know which way to turn the steering wheel.

"Well, the officers all jumped out of the car and ran to the Roadster and started to try to get to me. Mr. Poe told them to stop, that I was HIS prisoner, having already surrendered to him, but they grabbed me and put handcuffs on me anyway.

"They started to shove me into their car before one of them even saw the gun in my pocket. He grabbed it quick, and took it away, telling later that he had disarmed me while I was still in the car, but that wasn't so.

"They took me to Kingsport to the police station there, and there was a mob already waiting. We went inside, and they shoved me down in a chair along the side of the wall, and a lot of people crowded through there, looking at me like I was some kind of a sideshow in the circus. There was a window about eight or ten feet away, and a teenage boy was trying to climb through it, but all he got in was his head and shoulders the room was so crowded.

"A big pot-bellied dentist from there in Kingsport, Dr. Hutchins, came up and started cussing me and calling me all sorts of vile names. He spat in my face! I was handcuffed, my arms behind me, and could only try to dodge. I asked the officers near me to stop that man from what he was doing, or let me loose long enough to stop him myself, and they finally pulled him away. I told him that some day he might be sorry he had spit in my face.

"After that, they took me to Blountville, the county seat of Sullivan County, and locked me up in jail. They didn't treat me too badly up there, it was better than it had been in Kingsport, and they let a couple of lawyers, Burrows and Warren, come and talk to me. They said my Dad had asked them to represent me in my trial.

"The trial was held the next week, and the courthouse was so pack-jammed with people there were no seats and no standing room. In fact, there were great numbers of people standing in the halls and outside, near the windows and doors, trying to see or hear what was going on.

"Well, anyway, they had my trial there, and they convicted me real quick. They asked me on the witness stand if I was sorry that I had killed those officers. I told them the truth, that I was sorry that I HAD to kill them. If I hadn't shot them, they would have shot and killed me, just like the officers down in Mississippi tried to do.

"Well, they sentenced me to the electric chair, but my lawyers managed to point out that some new witnesses had been found who saw the shootout at the river, and besides, they hadn't really had ample time to prepare for the trial, and the judge agreed, and granted a new trial.

"They took me to Knoxville, to jail there for a while, and during that time they accused my kid brother, Kelsey, of smuggling a gun in to me, and they arrested him and tried him over that, and gave him a year in jail.

161

"After that, they took me back to Blountville, to stay until my new trial started, and I learned right away that they meant to try to kill me before the trial ever took place. I heard a couple of deputies talking about how they would let me escape and shoot me down. They planned to put me in a cell by myself and leave it unlocked so I would just walk out of it.

"So, I got Bert Davenport, who was a prisoner in the jail with me, and some other fellows, and we planned an escape of our own, before the deputies could act on their plan.

"We piled a couple of the thin mattresses up against the cell door and set them on fire. The heat against the metal bars made them swell, of course, so we used a cot frame to pry against the door and it popped right open. When the jailer came in with prisoners he had been using for road work, Bert hit him over the head with a pop bottle and we grabbed his guns and keys.

"Me and Bert and five or six others ran out of the jail, and nobody tried to stop us. I understand that later a lot of deputies and guards and even the jailers wife claim they shot at us, but I didn't see or hear any one do any shooting. Me and Bert headed toward the Virginia line, and the other boys scattered in all directions.

"Blountville is only a few miles cross country from Virginia, so we made it in a few hours. I understand that the lawmen searched all over Sullivan County and Kingsport for us, but we were long gone. "I hid out for a while, visiting friends and relatives, and even went back to Kingsport a few times, but they never caught me. I stayed around there for a while, raising a little money so I could come West. I even worked in a mine for a time, riding over there once a week with a couple of friends from Kingsport and coming back with them on weekends.

"When I had enough money saved up, I come out here, to Arkansas, and got work on a farm.

"Sunday afternoon was the only time I had off, and I would wander around and see the countryside on those times. Yesterday, I came on this barn, where a bunch of men were gathered. I went in to see what was going on, and they were playing cards and drinking. They gave me a drink or two, and asked me to join the game. I had a few dollars, so I did.

"And I won a couple of hands. This one fellow, William Carper they called him, started losing, and got mad about it. He would fuss and cuss, and he started getting mean. A kid walked in to the barn about that time, and Carper jumped up and started slapping him

162

around. I told him to pick on somebody his own size, and he hit me. I hit back and we went at it hard and heavy for a while. I was getting the best of him, I think, but his brother Sam grabbed a swingletree from the harness rack on the wall and hit me over the head with it and knocked me out.

"When I came to, I looked around and my gun was laying there beside my hand and the two Carper Brothers were laying there, shot to death. I truly don't know if I killed them. I don't remember it at all. I may have. Or someone else could have killed them and put the gun down beside me. I don't know. But they are dead.

"Some of the boys there told me that this county had a woman sheriff, and I don't fight with women. So I came in to surrender to you."

Sheriff Barber shook her head in wonderment. She had never heard such a tale before, and believed the young man to be truthful and sincere.

"What am I going to DO with him?" she asked herself. "If I send him back to Tennessee, they'll electrocute him. If I keep him for trial here, the Carpers' friends will testify against him and they'll give him the death sentence."

She studied long and hard about the problem, and finally decided what to do.

She turned him over to the state of Mississippi to stand trial for that first killing two years earlier on Christmas day.

Alone, with no one to defend him, and unable to afford an attorney, Knnie Wagner was tried in Mississippi for the killing of Deputy Sheriff Murdock MacIntosh.

He was convicted on that charge, the only conviction other than the one in Blountville for the two officers' deaths that he ever received. And, to the disappointment of the Greene County Sheriff, was not given the death penalty, but sentenced to life imprisonment in Parchman Penitentiary, Mississippi's notorious penal institution.

Contrary to expectations, Kinnie gave his guards no trouble. He was a hard worker, never complained or faked sickness, and had no trouble with other prisoners. His reputation had preceded him, even behind the walls and bars, and the prison-toughs and bullies gave him a wide berth.

Bored and tired of prison life, overworked and hopeless of his future, Kinnie saw a chance to run away one day in 1927, and did so. He made it to a cottonfield shack and obtained a gun from the resident, but, after a brief shootout in which he was hopelessly outnumbered, he surrendered. After a few weeks in solitary confinement, Kinnie decided to play the game of model prisoner.

Mississippi had a strange prison system in those days. Trustees, prisoners who had proven themselves to be trustworthy, were made guards over the other convicts, and were even given guns!

Weeks turned into months and months dragged on into years, and one day, Kinnie found himself accepting duty as an armed guard, complete with high-powered rifle and ammunition!

The farmlands and cottonfields surrounding the prison complex were a favorite hideout for escaped prisoners, most of whom had only wanted a short visit home rather than a fullfledged prison break as sometimes portrayed in the movies.

Kinnie had little trouble rounding up these men. They came back to the walls and cells willingly, having found that things at home were no longer as pleasant as they had supposed or remembered.

Several times the warden commended Wagner for his outstanding devotion to duty. Newspapermen wrote stories about him. And, in both the hills of Virginia and East Tennessee and the cottonlands around Parchman, a new song began to catch on:

The Kinnie Wagner Song
(author unknown; written about 1927)

"I'm sure you've heard the story
called the Kinnie Wagner Song
How down in Mississippi
I took the road that was wrong.

"It was down in Mississippi
where I shot my first man,
when the Sheriff there at Leaksville
for justice took a stand.

"Then I went from Mississippi
to the state of Tennessee,
Two men went down before me,
and they took my liberty.

"I wandered through the country
but I never could find rest
till I came to Texarkana,
a way out in the west.

"Again I started drinking
and again I pulled my gun,
and within a single moment,
the deadly work was done.

"The sheriff was a woman,
but she got the drop on me,
I quit the game and surrendered,
gave up my liberty.

"Now I'm down in Mississippi,
and I soon shall know my fate,
I'm waiting for the trial,
but I do not fear the case.

For still the sun is shining
and the sky is blue and fair,
My heart is not regaining,
for I do not fear the chair.

"Young boys, young boys take warning,
Oh, take my last advice:
If you start the game in life wrong,
you will surely pay the price."

Guitars twanged and fiddles wailed, and many a man and woman hummed the catchy tune under their breath as they worked, perhaps singing a few lines of the verses now and then, never stopping to consider how many mistakes and discrepancies the lyrics contained.

According to Kinnie, the sheriff at Leaksville never took any stand for "justice" but only for graft, corruption, and personal gain.

And when they "took my liberty" in Tennessee, the song mentioned nothing about his escape from jail nor his flight to avoid prosecution, but simply had him "wandering through the country" until

165

he went "way out west" to Arkansas, just across the big river from Tennessee!

The "woman sheriff" never "got the drop" on Wagner, he walked in and surrendered voluntarily. But the song made a hit anyhow. I got kind of tired of hearing it myself.

In 1941, when we got word that Kinnie had escaped from Parchman Prison a second time, everyone figured he would head back to Scott County, where he could hide out in relative safety. Relative safety, because he had so many relations over there. Come to think of it, he had a lot of kin in and around Kingsport as well, and most of them were perfectly willing to hide him or help him in any way they could.

During this time, I was still hauling paper and such for the newspaper when they called me, providing I could work it in among other jobs, which I usually could do if I tried. Other driving and hauling jobs come along with pleasing regularity, too, and the stash of cash I had hidden in an old sock in a certain place, never mind where, grew impressively.

One day, the editor of the paper called me. "Pug," he said, "I've got a job for you if you want it." "You need some more paper hauled from Bristol?" I asked.

"No, this is a driving job. I need you to drive over to the coalfields in Virginia. There's been a report that Knnie Wagner is hiding out over there, and we need to send a reporter to do a story on it. I'll send a reporter and a photographer with you, but I'd rather you drove them, because you know the roads and the territory and they don't. They could get lost and never get out of those hills."

"I can believe that," I told him. "I heard of a traveling salesman who went over in that territory to make a circuit of the company stores. He was over there so long the company he worked for had gone broke and was out of business before he got his last order shipped."

The mine where Wagner was reportedly hiding out was high in the Virginia mountains, near the Kentucky state line. I had been there once a long time earlier, and figured I could find it without too much trouble.

We set out early the following morning. The editor had chosen a young fellow as a photographer who looked like he could climb mountains alright. He was a long-legged galoot, tall and skinny, and he carried that big Speed Graphex camera slung across his shoulder in such a way that it made him kind of tilt to one side when he walked.

166

The reporter was a young woman, kind of stringy-haired and plain, with thick-lens glasses perched on her nose. She started giving me orders right away.

"Don't drive too fast," she said. "I get car sick. Especially going around curves."

"There's a bucket there in the floorboard at the back seat," I told her. "I don't want to cause you no problem, but I'm working for your boss, not you. He told me to hurry, so you just hang on."

Well, she didn't like that none too much, but I didn't spend much time worrying about it. At least she didn't try giving me any more orders.

We got over to the mine country before noon, after a hard drive through the winding mountain roads of Southwest Virginia.

Scott, Wise and Lee counties don't look all that big on a map, but if you could flatten them out, they'd be danged near as big as Texas.

The newspaper gal didn't get sick after all, and I took some of the curves at a right good clip of speed, especially the few times we were going down hill. It's uphill most of the way going over there, but it's down hill most of the way coming back.

The mining camp consisted of a company store and a couple of dozen clapboard or frame cottages, built on posts for foundation supports, scattered along the side of a mountain.

We had hardly got out of the car and unloosened our stiff bodies, cramped as they were from the long drive, when there was a loud "Whoosh!" sound, and dust and smoke blew out the mine entrance.

"Cave in!" somebody hollered, and people came running from everywhere.

Somebody started beating on a pan or gong or something, making a loud enough noise to wake up half the folks in the county, it seemed, then a warning siren started wailing.

I looked up toward the office shack beside the company store, and there was a fellow out there turning a hand crank siren, its mournful wailing rising and failing like the cry of the fabled Irish Banshee.

"Oh, my God!" the reporter girl said. "Get pictures, Frank. This is going to be a real story!"

Well, it figured. Everybody else was worried about the cave in, and about men that might be trapped inside the collapsed mine, and this here female writer type was busy worrying about writing up the story about it all.

167

But I got to give her credit. She didn't get in the way too much, and she got the information she was after.

The photographer got busy snapping pictures of the mine entrance and the people crowded around it. Some of the workmen ran to get picks and shovels, and they began digging out the mine entrance almost before we got up there where they were. I went up to see if I could help.

A plump man . . . . not fat, but plump ... seemed to be in charge. He wore a sweat-stained white shirt under his suit coat and vest. His tie had been pulled loose to give him plenty of air. He was handing out picks and shovels, and giving all kinds of orders.

"I don't think it's too bad," he said. "There are only four of the men back there near the elevator, and I think the cave in is up here, near the front. If we get it cleared fast, they'll be alright."

He handed me a shovel, and I went over to the pile of rubble in the entrance and started helping to clear it away.

It didn't take too long. I wasn't an expert by any means when it came to using that kind of hand digging tools, but in an emergency like that, I wanted to help all I could.

Those miners and their wives ... I didn't tell you that, but the women pitched in just like men, using shovels and picks and wheelbarrows to clear the mine entrance . . . some of them really could move the dirt. Or rock. Or whatever it may be.

Before long, enough of the blocked area had been cleared so we could see a little opening at the top. The plump man in the wilted suit came up and climbed up as far as he could on the rubble and hollered over it. "Hello, inside the mine! Can you hear me?"

"Yes!" came a faint voice from inside the carved cavern. "We're all alright. We're digging away at this side and we'll soon be clear."

Everyone breathed a sigh of relief when we heard that. There were no injuries, apparently, and no fatalities.

By the time we got the entrance cleared enough to let the miners out, they had been joined by six others who had been working back in the shafts when the cave-in occurred. They all came out, grinning broadly and squinting in the sunlight as they wiped the black coal dust from their faces.

The reporter gal got her story, but not the one she had wanted.

"I'm going to write this up and telephone it in," she told me. "This can't wait until we drive all the way back."

She went off somewhere and was gone for a half hour. When she came back, she looked downright pleased with herself. "It's finished," she told the photographer. "And I think it's good. Listen to this:

"God was present on a high Virginia mountain this day when ten coal miners narrowly escaped the horrible fate of being buried alive. He looked down on the scene with pity, and allowed rescuers to clear the caved-in rubble from the mine entrance. . ."

"Sounds good," the photographer said. She hurried off to the company store to find a telephone.

"I'm sorry," the commissary man told her, "but the telephone is out. Line must be down somewhere on the mountain. But we got a telegraph, and I can operate it. I can send it that way for you if you like."

"Fine," the reporter said. "Send this word for word." She gave him the papers with her story written on it and told him the address and all, and he got right on it. The clickety-clack of the telegraph key sounded for some time.

The reporter gal kind of strutted around among the mine folks, telling them about her story and how she thought they would like it.

Ten minutes later, the telegraph key began to clack again, with a reply coming in.

The operator got it all down and read it to us.

"FORGET ABOUT KINNIE WAGNER" it said. "FORGET ABOUT CAVE-IN. FORGET ABOUT MINE. GET PICTURE OF GOD AND IF POSSIBLE ARRANGE INTERVIEW. EDITOR."

In 1940, fifteen years after the episode in Arkansas, the newspapers had another story:

"Tune up that Guitar, Willie...Kinnie Is Outlawin' Again (by Nea Service)

"Kinnie Wagner, one of those killers who inspire men in mountain cabins to tune the old guitar and make up songs, is at large again.

"Somewhere around northwestern Mississippi and Arkansas, the bushy-haired, beetle-browed gunman who had killed at least five men has the authorities once more on his trail. Before they find him there ought to be several more stanzas added to the hillbilly near-classic "Kinnie Wagner Was His Name".

Gory but Gallant

"Wagner first earned immortality in song among the Tennessee hillbillies by shooting two peace officers. He had practiced for this feat by running away from his Virginia home and joining a circus, where he became a crack shot. He left the circus at Meridian, Miss., in 1924, and while working at lumber jacking found himself in the Lucedale jail for petty larceny.

"He obtained a saw, cut his cell bars, slugged the jailer who was bringing him his breakfast, and escaped. For nearly a month he was a fugitive, but on Christmas Eve, 1924, he mowed down with shotguns two deputy sheriffs who knocked on the door of his hideout. He got away.

"For four months Wagner was a shadow, appearing briefly in this city or that, then vanishing.

But on April 13, 1924, a deputy and a policeman were shot to death, and a second policeman badly wounded in answering a complaint of a disturbance near Kingsport, Tenn. Wagner's arrest followed the next day at Blountville and he was promptly sentenced to be electrocuted. An appeal to the Tennessee Supreme Court saved him this time, and while awaiting a new trial, Wagner improved his time by escaping from jail.

"I gave up because I was tired of being hounded like a dog", said Wagner, possibly thinking of another verse for the ballad. "When I saw that a woman was leading the posse, I threw in the sponge. I don't fight against women. " You could almost hear the cords of the guitar, Wagner being fresh from the murder of two friends in a fight the night before.

"His record qualified Wagner to become a trustee, which status he enjoyed for several years. He justified his jailers' leniency and confidence the other day. Forcing a convict camp driver to take him out of the prison camp in a prison car, he stole the driver's clothes and the car, set him afoot, and vanished."

This was in October, 1940, and Kinnie Wagner's taste of freedom was to last for three years.

The "convict camp driver" mentioned in the NEA story was Sgt. J. C. Fowler, a Mississippi prison guard who had earned a reputation for his harsh treatment of convict workmen.

Fowler wasn't harmed, physically, but his ego was badly bruised, and he had a lot of explaining to do to a Mississippi legislative committee who came to Parchman penitentiary to investigate the escape.

John Baswell of Oktibbeha County identified before the committee two penitentiary employees and a convict trustee as the three men who visited him the night after Wagner's escape, seeking a letter Wagner had written.

The letter was written by Wagner, before his escape, to a former convict. Mystery shrouds its contents, some contending it sought aid for escaping, others that it was simply a letter asking the former convict to join Wagner in a dove hunt.

The charges were denied by the men, Sgts. A. C. Wells, J.C. Fowler and J.C. Dixon.

Some folks speculated that the letter actually contained a report of considerable wrong doing and graft at the prison, and exposed several officials and aides on the warden's staff.

For most of a year, in 1941, Kinnie Wagner hid out, the FBI later reported, around Luka and Corinth in northeast Mississippi.

Two negroes were killed in that area during that period of time, and Wagner was considered a suspect in the deaths.

He was captured in his native Scott County, not far from Bristol, Virginia, in 1943, and taken to the Bristol City Jail.

Worley Fleenor, a Methodist preacher who had grown up in Kingsport and who had been present every day at Wagner's Blountville trial, wrote a letter to the prisoner while he was yet confined in Bristol jail, before his return to Parchman.

In part, the letter explained that the writer, now Reverend Fleenor, had been present at the Kingsport jail when Wagner was brought in, after his surrender and capture following the shootout at Holston River. Rev. Fleenor was the teenaged youth who had managed to get his head and shoulders through an open window near where the young desperado had been seated.

"I saw that dentist spit in your face," he related, "and I heard the vile names he called you." The preacher also sent along a New Testament, in hopes, he said, that it might help Kinnie find peace and relief from some of his troubles.

After being returned to Parchman, Wagner began a regular correspondence with the preacher. Many letters were exchanged over the following years, and the two men became fast friends.

Wagner wrote out his entire story and sent it to Reverend Fleenor, telling him to use it in any way he could to help young men and try to keep them from making the same mistakes he had made.

"I long for the day," Kinnie wrote," that I might be pardoned, and be able to go to schools and churches and talk to young men and advise them on how to avoid temptations and stay out of trouble."

He began a Bible class there in prison, trying to teach other prisoners something of what he had now read and learned.

Guards and some prisoners sniggered, but only behind his back. He was, after all, still considered the fastest gun in the South, and had twice proven that he could escape the prison any time he really wanted to do so.

Within a few months, Kinnie Wagner was again made trustee, and given back his job as armed guard.

In that position, he could often leave the prison for weekends, looking for convicts who had run off. As long as he reported back by Monday morning, he was free to roam the Mississippi cottonfields on Saturdays and Sundays.

The warden, realizing that Wagner needed to revisit his old home and family back in Virginia, granted him several furloughs, or leaves, notably around the Christmas holiday seasons.

World War II raged in Europe and in the Pacific, and Wagner begged to be allowed to go fight.

"I've never done anything but bring shame and disgrace upon my country, upon my people," he wrote Rev. Fleenor, "but I'd like to do something. If I could go to Germany or Japan or anywhere and fight, and give my life for my country, and save some mother's son or some woman's husband, I'd be happy to go and die for my country and give my life if I could."

He asked the preacher to talk to the Selective Service Board and see if there was anyway they might let him go into the Army or Navy.

The board was adamant. No one with a criminal record, and certainly no one serving a life sentence for murder, could be inducted into any branch of military service.

Victory finally came in Europe, and at last, after the atomic bomb devastated two cities, Japan surrendered. The war was over.

In 1945, Wagner was given a two-week furlough. He visited Kingsport and his family in Speers Ferry, Virginia, and, reportedly, even visited one of the family members of one of the officers he had killed that fateful day on the banks of the Holston River. During the ensuing years, he was given 9 more leaves of absence from Parchman, to visit his folks in Virginia, unescorted! "Stone walls do not a prison make," a poet says, "nor iron bars make a cage". That may be true, but confinement, hampered movement and absence of freedom tell on even the strongest personality, and the iron will of Kinnie Wagner

172

once again began to weaken, hungering for the unreserved liberty he had briefly, and seldom, once known.

On March 15, 1948, he escaped from Parchman one last time.

That made a total of six escapes, from the time he first fled the vengeful sheriff in Leaksville, Mississippi, just after Christmas Day in 1924. He escaped from the shootout scene at Holston River, only to surrender the following day. He escaped from Blountville jail, and remained at large for more than a year, until he gave himself up following the dual killings of the Carper brothers in Arkansas. He escaped three times from Parchman Penitentiary, and this last time, remained free and at large, evading the law for seven years!

He took with him the high-powered rifle he had used as a trustee guard, prompting the FBI to warn that he was armed and dangerous on their "most wanted" list.

Well known as Mississippi's most wanted killer and most renowned escape artist, Kinnie Wagner stayed with friends in both Mississippi and Virginia during those years. He often visited Kingsport, and was frequently an overnight guest in the homes of relatives there.

But at last, on January 29, 1956, a posse of Highway Patrolmen cornered him near Scooba in Kemper County, and he surrendered one last time.

Within months, he was again made trustee. Doctors had detected a heart problem, and Kinnie knew he could no longer bear the strain of being a hunted man, nor could he work as hard as previously in searching for run-offs and escaped prisoners.

He decided to try to train dogs to assist him in his efforts. He was given a German Shepherd female to work with, and soon had her obeying his commands as well as the movie dog Rin-Tin-Tin.

Kinnie decided to breed the dog, and train the puppies as well.

But he suffered a slight heart attack just before the puppies were born. The doctors ordered him hospitalized, and he was taken to the prison infirmary.

Like an expectant father, he fretted and fumed and worried when birth time came.

The litter of pups was born on Saturday night. Kinnie got word the following day, and asked if he could be temporarily released to go see about them.

The dog and her puppies were out at Camp 6, some little distance from the main prison.

Assistant Supt. E. E. Lacy agreed to take Wagner out there in his car. The once feared desperado was now a grey-haired, aging man of 54, although he remained tall and straight and sturdy.

They drove through the piney woods to Camp 6, talking of the puppies and Wagner's plans to train them

Once there, they hurried to the kennel where the dog was kept.

"Oh, look at these beauties!" Wagner said, petting the mother dog as he examined the newborn pups.

"Come and look!" he called to E.H. Sanders, Jr., the Camp Inventory Clerk.

He held up one of the tiny creatures as Sanders walked up.

Suddenly, a grimace twisted his rugged face. He grasped at his chest and pitched forward, landing face down on the floor. The puppy, still in his hand, was safely cushioned from the fall. Sanders and Lacy quickly dropped to their knees beside the fallen man. Lacy grabbed his wrist and felt for a pulse.

"Go call for an ambulance," he told Sanders.

"I think he's had another heart attack."

Kinnie Wagner was pronounced dead at 3:45 p.m. that day, Sunday, March 9, 1958, just three months past the 34th anniversary of that first killing on Christmas Eve, 1924. Although he had killed at least five men, he had won and kept the loyalty and love of many friends and kinsmen who had known the full story, and who were convinced, beyond doubt, that his deadly aim and marksmanship had been used only in self defense.

They took the body back to Scott County, to a funeral home at Weber City, not far from his old Speers Ferry home.

The Scott County Funeral Home reported that "at least 10,000 people" came to view the body as it lay in an open coffin there.

That figure was later revised to 15,000.

Cars packed both sides of the highway, all the way from Gate City to Kingsport, across the state line in Tennessee.

Employees at the funeral home were kept busy trying to keep the long lines of viewers under control, and they ran out of visitor's registers to be signed.

The final chapter in the life of Kinnie Wagner closed late Wednesday afternoon at a secluded cemetery on a hillside overlooking the Southwest Virginia mountains he had roamed and loved.

A small portion of the huge crowd of people who had viewed the body followed all the way to the little Mountain View School Cemetery just outside Gate City on the way to Nickelsville.

The coffin was opened for the last time just before it was lowered into a grave beside that of the mother he had lost so long ago. Friends of the gunman again moved forward for a final memory, then stepped back, many of them wiping tears from their eyes.

Automobiles, many from Mississippi where Wagner had died in the state penitentiary Sunday, blocked the winding mountain road leading from State Route 71 to the cemetery.

It was over at last. Kinnie Wagner had made his last escape, and this time would never be recaptured.

www.ingramcontent.com/pod-product-compliance
Lightning Source LLC
Chambersburg PA
CBHW022108280326
41933CB00007B/306